Theory and Practice in Library Education

RESEARCH STUDIES IN LIBRARY SCIENCE
Bohdan S. Wynar, Editor

No. 1. *Middle Class Attitudes and Public Library Use.* By Charles Evans, with an Introduction by Lawrence Allen.

No. 2. *Critical Guide to Catholic Reference Books.* 2nd ed. By James Patrick McCabe, with an Introduction by Russell E. Bidlack.

No. 3. *An Analysis of Vocabulary Control in Library of Congress Classification and Subject Headings.* By John Phillip Immroth, with an Introduction by Jay E. Daily.

No. 4. *Research Methods in Library Science. A Bibliographic Guide.* By Bohdan S. Wynar.

No. 5. *Library Management: Behavior-Based Personnel Systems. A Framework for Analysis.* By Robert E. Kemper.

No. 6. *Computerizing the Card Catalog in the University Library: A Survey of User Requirements.* By Richard P. Palmer, with an Introduction by Kenneth R. Shaffer.

No. 7. *Toward a Philosophy of Educational Librarianship.* By John M. Christ.

No. 8. *Freedom Versus Suppression and Censorship.* By Charles H. Busha, with an Introduction by Peter Hiatt, and a Preface by Allan Pratt.

No. 9. *The Role of the State Library in Adult Education: A Critical Analysis of Nine Southeastern State Library Agencies.* By Donald D. Foos, with an Introduction by Harold Goldstein.

No. 10. *The Concept of Main Entry as Represented in the Anglo-American Cataloging Rules. A Critical Appraisal with Some Suggestions: Author Main Entry vs. Title Main Entry.* By M. Nabil Hamdy, with an Introduction by Jay E. Daily.

No. 11. *Publishing in Switzerland: The Press and the Book Trade.* By Linda S. Kropf.

No. 12. *Library Science Dissertations, 1925-1972: An Annotated Bibliography.* By Gail A. Schlachter and Dennis Thomison.

No. 13. *Milestones in Cataloging: Famous Catalogers and Their Writings; 1835-1969.* By Donald J. Lehnus, with an Introduction by Phyllis A. Richmond.

No. 14. *Weeding Library Collections.* By Stanley J. Slote.

No. 15. *Library of Congress Subject Headings: Principles and Application.* By Lois Mai Chan.

No. 16. *Theory and Practice in Library Education: The Teaching-Learning Process.* By Joe Morehead.

Theory and Practice in Library Education

The Teaching-Learning Process

Joe Morehead

Libraries Unlimited, Inc.   1980
Littleton, Colorado

LIBRARIES UNLIMITED, INC.
P.O. Box 263
Littleton, Colorado 80160

Library of Congress Cataloging in Publication Data

Morehead, Joe, 1931-
    Theory and practice in library education.

    (Research studies in library science ; no. 16)
    Bibliography: p. 125
    Includes index.
    1. Library education. I. Title. II. Series.
Z674.R4 no. 16 [Z668]   020s   [020'.7]
ISBN 0-87287-215-7   80-17431

TABLE OF CONTENTS

Introduction 7

1 — Professional Education 11
Introduction 11
Professional Schools in a University Setting 12
Theory versus Practice in Professional Education 14
Comparative Trends in Professional Education 15
    Medical Education 16
    Engineering Education 17
    Legal Education 18
    Social Work Education 19
    Teacher Education 20
Criteria for Integrating Theory and Practice 22
Summary 24
References 25

2 — Library Education 29
Introduction 29
The Library School and the University Environment 30
Theory and Practice in Library Education 32
    Williamson 33
    Reece 35
    From Reece to the Present 37
Summary 46
References 50

3 — Modes of Instruction in Library Education 54
Introduction 54
Categories of Instruction 55
    Face-to-Face Instruction 55
    Independent Study 56
Applications 57
    Class Presentation 57
    Problems 62
        Supervised Independent Study, 62; Unsupervised
        Independent Study, 63

3 — Modes of Instruction in Library Education
Applications (cont'd)
Observation 64
Projects 65
Laboratory Work 67
Summary 71
References 75

4 — Library-Centered Library Education 79
Introduction 79
The Library-Centered Library School 80
The Content of Library-Centered Library Education 81
Library-Centered Teaching Methods 82
Knapp and the Teaching-Learning Process 83
The Library School Library As Laboratory 84
Theoretical Justification 88
Learning Strategies in Library-Centered Library Education 90
Critical Incident Theory 91
Dewey's Inquiry Model 93
Teaching Strategies in Library-Centered Library Education 95
Action Research 95
Participant Observation 96
The Inquiry Model and Critical Incident 98
Summary 99
References 102

5 — Toward a Resolution of Theory and Practice 107
Introduction 107
The Information Component in the Theory-Practice Equation 109
Suggestions, Reflections, Conclusions 113
Freedom, Relevance, and Discovery 117
References 121

Selected Bibliography 125

Personal Author Index 135

Subject Index 137

INTRODUCTION

This study is an exploration of a perennial issue in professional education generally and library education specifically: the problem of theory and practice in the instructional process. Basic to a resolution of principles and techniques in education for librarianship is the need to articulate a conceptual framework for self-appropriated learning so that an understanding of theory, grounded in practical tasks, arises from the logical processes of a secure and reliable pedagogy. The work is intended for library educators, their students, and practicing professionals who have had an opportunity to apply to the tasks at hand the theory they have learned in school.

Chapter 1 of this study addresses the problem of theory and practice in selected professions. A brief account of medical, engineering, legal, social work, and teacher education serves to exemplify the universality of concern over the appropriate admixture of theory and operations in professional curricula. Chapter 2 examines library education specifically. Out of my own uneasiness with much of the discussion surrounding the theory-practice issue, I have been constrained to return to the early theoreticians of library education, Williamson and Reece, and have found that their insights hold up remarkably well. In Chapter 3 I have drawn upon a large body of research into the teaching-learning process in fashioning an account of the several modes of instruction and their potential application in resolving the theory-practice problem. Chapter 4 examines the merits of library-centered library education and its enabling methodologies of action research, participant observation, and John Dewey's inquiry model. The final chapter assays the resolution of theory and practice within the context of information studies and current technologies. My conclusions and suggestions argue for a teaching-learning strategy that emphasizes student-centered, heuristic activity. The whole comprises a philosophical essay about these critical issues, intended not so much as a blueprint for specific change but as a stimulus to further research, ideas to be forged and tested in the educational crucible.

The somewhat baffling nature and persistence of the theory-practice issue is, I suspect, a function of something deeply embedded in human nature: the craving for unity. This reductive desire, a manifestation of what Lovejoy called "metaphysical pathos," has enjoyed a long tenure in the tradition of Western philosophy, and in one of its mundane forms is exemplified in the idea of a unitary teaching mode free from the "troublesome cleavages and disjunctions of things."[1] Indeed, so strong is the passion for unity that some philosophers thought the ideal was actually realized. Augustine, for example, in his contrived dialogue with Adeodatus, would have us believe "that in speaking we desire only that we may teach."[2]

The susceptibility to this kind of metaphysical pathos has discouraged, perhaps foredoomed, successful attempts at significant curricular innovation in large part because such efforts are untidy, stumbling, disorderly, often confusing and frustrating. They require that we endeavor to manage diversity, accommodate many variables, risk time and energy. How much easier it has been to avoid this vexatious multiplicity and transmit knowledge in the traditional manner as if our students possessed one collective mind. It is tempting to avoid the difficulties of reconciling theory and practice because resolution partakes of the unruly nature of the real world. To incorporate the experiential component into our modes of instruction threatens the comfortable security of traditional teaching-learning strategies in the pedagogical enterprise. We fear the reality of Tennyson's metaphor of experience as "an arch wherethro'/Gleams that untravell'd world whose margin fades/For ever and for ever when I move."[3]

The majority of writers who discuss theory and practice do not define their use of those words but rely upon the reader to comprehend the sense conveyed in the context of their remarks. Accordingly, those characteristics of an instructional program that are implied when a library school claims "to emphasize theory rather than practice" include synonymously related terms used freely and interchangeably. Few commentators on the theory-practice problem have suggested that either word has a singular, indissoluble meaning. Consequently, the synonymously related terms are used to convey similar emphases, a recognizable pattern of what Wittgenstein called "family resemblances."[4]

The authoritative reference sources reflect the commodious nature of the terms, and the search for precision founders in tautological circumlocution. *Webster's Third New International Dictionary of the English Language* equates theory with "principle or plan of action" and offers five definitions that purport to reflect contemporary usage. *The Random House Dictionary of the English Language* stresses the colloquial relationship of theory and hypothesis, defining the former as "a more or less verified or established explanation accounting for known facts or phenomena." *The Oxford English Dictionary* among its many definitions represents theory as "a systematic statement of rules or principles to be followed."

The words "practice" and "practical" also enjoy a range of synonymously related terms, but, in the writings cited in this study, appear to be more amenable to circumscribed meanings. However, as I point out in Chapter 2, both Williamson and Reece descried a certain insouciance in the way library educators were using these terms during the 1920s and 1930s. Moreover, many writers, in contrasting theory and practice, have used the latter pejoratively, and this cavalier distinction has tended to generate more heat than light in the efforts to reconcile the two.

If the absence of terminological specificity suggests the reality of usage, it is important to accept this fact. I have endeavored in this study to acknowledge that reality and to use synonymously related terms to describe the theoretical and practical components. For the former, related general terms include principles, concepts, formulations, propositions, assumptions, and working hypotheses; for the latter, skills, processes, operations, and techniques. Where in a specific context some nuance in terminology is warranted, a distinction has been so indicated.

Theory and practice as a problem in library education generated a great deal of discussion in earlier decades, but has been relatively neglected in the 1970s, if one can judge by the paucity of debate in the library literature. If the 1975 Delphi-Method survey is an accurate indication of interest among library educators, the theory-practice question is perceived as having little cogency. While there was support for "the inclusion of practical experience, field study, internship, etc. in the master's program," few were optimistic "about such experiences being included in the curriculum."[5] Reasons for this apathy are considered in Chapter 5 of this study, but the theory-practice mix as an issue will not vanish simply by wishful indifference on the part of library educators. It is my hope that this prolusion will serve to revive the moribund interest in the resolution of the problem, a pursuit that continues to be worthy of sustained, disciplined inquiry.

REFERENCES

[1]Arthur O. Lovejoy, *The Great Chain of Being* (New York: Harper and Row, 1960), p. 13.

[2]George C. Leckie (trans.), *De Magistro*, by St. Aurelius Augustine (New York: D. Appleton-Century Co., 1938), p. 3.

[3]Alfred, Lord Tennyson, "Ulysses."

[4]G. E. M. Anscombe (trans.), *Philosophical Investigations*, by Ludwig Wittgenstein (Oxford: Basil Blackwell, 1953), sects. 66-67.

[5]Kenneth E. Vance et al., "Future of Library Education: 1975 Delphi Study," *Journal of Education for Librarianship*, 18 (Summer, 1977), 7-8.

1

PROFESSIONAL EDUCATION

INTRODUCTION

Professional education, according to McGlothlin, is "the most complex and difficult of all forms of higher education. Professional schools cannot be content merely with transmitting knowledge, although knowledge is important to them; they must make sure that the graduates are both knowledgeable and competent to practice."[1]

Broadly speaking, professional education includes "all that education which prepares for professional calling or employment. It may be differentiated on the one hand from vocational education, which relates to those employments not generally recognized as professions, and on the other hand from general and liberal education which has no specific practical application in view."[2] But even liberal education aims partly at assisting the graduate to gain a livelihood, whereas the "academic" part of vocational education is increasingly handled by the burgeoning community college system.

Flexner's famous and influential study of medical education in 1910 set the tone of discussion for over half a century on professionalism and the proper education for professional activity.[3] Five years later, in attempting to determine whether the field of social work had achieved professional status, Flexner established six criteria for distinguishing professions from other occupations. In his analysis, professional activity was basically intellectual; it was learned, being predicated on a store of knowledge rather than routine; it was practical, in the sense of ultimately serving social ends; it was strongly organized internally; it was motivated by altruism; and its technique could be taught.[4]

Successive refinements of Flexner's definition show how well his criteria have endured. Carr-Saunders and Wilson, who wrote the most extensive single study of the professions, concluded that "the application of an intellectual technique to the ordinary business of life, acquired as a result of prolonged and specialized training, is the chief distinguishing characteristic of [a] profession."[5]

As this "prolonged and specialized training" became increasingly grounded in the American tradition of higher education, the terms "practical" and "technique" in Flexner's criteria were de-emphasized while the intellectual component was elevated. "Practical" training on a graduate level, it was said, debased the university, and, in fact, institutions of higher education that paid attention to the realities of the work world came to be labeled with the invidious term "trade school." Along with the "academic" versus "professional" argument came the problem of the place of theory and skills in the professional preparation of students.

PROFESSIONAL SCHOOLS
IN A UNIVERSITY SETTING

A good deal of the complexity and difficulty in McGlothlin's dictum arises from the kinds of arguments the subject generates. Debate is often acrimonious, and usually more heat than light is produced. As the universities gradually began to co-opt the professional schools, they asked that "the acquisition of professional skills and techniques amount to more than rituals or routines," and especially that these skills emphasize "the exercise of intelligence and judgment."[6] On the other hand, the alliance of universities and professional schools became a two-way street. Arguments at either end of this street are suspect, as is Hutchins' position, which contends that institutions of higher education provide solely the theoretical training and the professions the practical training needed for incoming members.[7] Similarly one-sided is the position of Bartky, who stated: "The ideal school of education finds no prototype in the academic departments of the university. Its offerings must be practical rather than theoretical; it must regulate its admissions on the basis of need; it must adjust its program to the student's convenience instead of making impractical demands in matters of residence, scheduling and course offerings; its academic standards must be flexible rather than rigid; and its research, at least for the time being, must aim at developing a valid approach."[8]

Both statements are obsolete. The university, perforce, is justified in asking that the theoretical foundations of professional practice be emphasized. It expects professional education "to be more than the transmission of an empirically derived body of knowledge and technique by persons who are themselves only professionally skilled."[9] However, "the professional school may legitimately expect the university to recognize that knowledge, understanding, and theoretical foundations are not enough for the professional practitioner, for he must also be a master of his craft. . . . It asks scholars in the fundamental disciplines to recognize that the standards that they ordinarily apply for evaluating scholarship may not always be pertinent for evaluating intellectual effort in professional fields."[10]

An attempt should be made to bring balance and perspective to a false dichotomy: the notion of an irreconcilable distinction between "graduate" and "professional" education. Studies of education for the various professions were given useful focus by Lloyd Blauch's compendium of accounts of thirty-four professional education programs.[11] Each account was prepared by a knowledgeable person in the field, and the study provided a checklist of the characteristics of the programs according to a common outline. Of the whole, the editor could say that, "students in graduate schools engage in highly specialized study in particular fields in which they will earn their living. There is ample justification, therefore, for regarding the graduate school as a professional school; perhaps it should be thought of as an undifferentiated professional school, since it offers preparation for a number of fields of work."[12]

But if the graduate school is an "undifferentiated" professional school, professional education "encompasses and exceeds" in its goals general undergraduate and graduate education. This is because "graduates of professional schools are instruments for the achievement of socially significant ends. They are not and cannot be ends in themselves alone." As McGlothlin pointed out, "the objectives of professional education include professional competence, certainly; but in addition they include social understanding, a professional personality which responds without conflict to the demands of professional ethics, zest for continued study, and ability to execute or interpret research."[13] These objectives are a restated version of Flexner's criteria, but their value as articulated goals provides a corrective to the dualism implicit in the arguments of Hutchins or Bartky.

Indeed, Berelson pointed out that it is useless to rail against the imputation of professional schools — with its unspoken modifier "narrow" — but rather one should equate specialization and professionalization in an acceptable definition of graduate work:

> As for the conception of graduate study as "academic" or "professional," I do not fear the latter so long as its meaning is clearly understood, i.e., that it does not necessarily mean the automatic acceptance or automatic rejection of proposals or practices in medicine, law or education. After all, the products of graduate school do *practice* a learned profession. Indeed, the graduate school is in the midst of a long movement in a professional direction that is not necessarily to be deplored but to be appreciated and exploited. The very increase of non-academic jobs for graduate school products has meant a decline in the exclusively *academic* character of the institution.[14]

It seems clear that nothing suggested in overcoming the division between academic and professional studies in a graduate setting condones low standards of intellectual effort and accomplishment, emphasis on trivial aspects of professional practice, disdain for fundamental knowledge, or concentration on skills to the sacrifice of scholarly pursuits. On the contrary, the conservative nature of the university provides the stability in which professional schools may attain intellectual stature. At the same time, "the schools help to keep the university dynamic, purposeful, responsive and responsible to the societies it ultimately serves."[15]

But to travel this two-way street is to encounter a dilemma, and this dilemma informs all attempts at experimentation and curriculum innovation. Ann Heiss, in her perceptive study on graduate schools, pointed out that "there have been practically no new ideas in the basic format of graduate study during the past three or four decades. If change by deletion occurs, it generally does so by default or as an unplanned consequence – for example, a professor resigns, retires or dies and 'his' course is dropped from the program."[16]

The problem seems to reside within the very structure of the institution. As McConnell says, "Because it is conservative, the university sometimes unduly restricts or curbs the development of sound professional programs. Without the sanctions which university scholars apply, however, it would be easy for the newer, exuberant professional schools to fail to maintain an appropriate balance between the general and the special, between the theoretical and the applied; and between what understanding and skill the student should acquire in the university and what knowledge and technique he should learn in an internship, apprenticeship, clerkship, or in the practice of the profession itself."[17]

If, as Heiss documented, real innovation is difficult to achieve in graduate education under the best circumstances, the teaching-learning ambience is hardly helped by futile debates over academic versus professional education. As Darley suggested, "the problem for graduate education now is not only to avoid a kind of professionalization so rigid that it strangles in its own curricular winding sheets . . . but, also, to foster a kind of professionalization that opens up new knowledge and new ways to make knowledge for the future."[18] Not only are arguments emphasizing the exclusivity of academic and professional areas counterproductive, but the implementing, via the curriculum, of programs designed to best prepare the aspirant to a professional career will never exceed a token effort.

THEORY VERSUS PRACTICE
IN PROFESSIONAL EDUCATION

The problem of "theory" versus "practice" in professional education appears in retrospect as an ineluctable consequence of the cooptation of professional schools within university settings. Professional service rests on mastery of a body of knowledge on the one hand and mastery of professional skills on the other. Anderson spoke of the desired "appropriate balance" of these two aspects of professional education: "Forces exist which would push professional education now one way, now the other. The forces in the educational environment, most frequently university forces, push for knowledge – knowledge which is derived from research and is rooted in and reinforced by theory. The forces emerging from practice push for craftsmanship of skill – the 'how we do it,' which is practice."[19]

Ironically, representatives of each position, in their calmer moments, "will acknowledge the necessary duality of education and training. But when decisions are to be made about curriculum or the locus of education (classroom, laboratory, clinic, or agency), contention often sets in again. Sometimes a truce is reached when one party says, 'I'll take two years, you take two.' But with new explosions of knowledge and the development of more elaborate skill, each tries to encroach on the time of the other. The dualisms of knowledge versus skill, theory versus practice, or basic versus applied will probably be with us always. *But these dualisms must be wrestled with continuously in professional education.*[20] (Emphasis added.)

Again, as in the extreme positions some educators take in the academic-professional argument, one may reject as undesirable the argument that *all* theory or *all* practice in a professional curriculum is the goal. As McGlothlin averred, "much of the conflict over professional schools centers around the curricula, mainly over whether the schools focus so sharply on 'vocational ends' that their graduates emerge, the accusation goes, as superb technicians but as poor scientists and poor citizens. The curricula of teacher education receive the brunt of this attack, but others are often included. Part of the attack is based on lack of understanding. No professional school I know of is interested in producing graduates who are trained so narrowly that they will be lost if a job requirement changes. Professional schools are just as aware as liberal arts colleges that society is dynamic and people mobile, and that the practice of a professional man may stretch over a period of forty-odd years during which much science and society may change."[21]

McGrath noted the obvious: "A plan for an ideal professional education cannot overlook the value of practical experience. Courses having to do with the techniques of daily practice . . . have in the past been prominent in all professional curricula."[22] Because professional education has the task of making certain that its graduates are competent to practice their professions, it places at least a modicum of emphasis on the skills of application. It does this by situating the student in a program being conducted by the profession, where he can work under supervision with increasing freedom and responsibility commensurate with demonstrated ability.

But if this is a fair statement of professional education's attempt to provide both theory and practice in its curricula, when one peruses the literature on education for the several professions, the picture is not as orderly as the statement implies.

COMPARATIVE TRENDS IN PROFESSIONAL EDUCATION

Writing over a decade ago, McGlothlin noted that "there are wide variations among the professions in their use of supervised work as a means of teaching the skills of application. Law has very little, if any, activity of this sort, depending almost wholly on later practice to bring command of these skills. Engineering, except within so-called cooperative programs where study on campus and work in industry alternate at set periods, does almost nothing. On the other hand, two years of medicine and dentistry are devoted to these activities, and medicine adds another year through the internship in hospitals, often directed by the medical school itself. Social work parallels classwork with field work, starting the latter within two weeks after entrance into the graduate school. But medicine and dentistry postpone the time for clinical training two full years after admission. Which is preferable? Or, even, why are there these large differences?"[23]

No concerted attempt has been made to discover what other professional educators outside the confines of one's own discipline are doing to grapple with these problems. Yet most students of professional training seem to recognize that the question is profound and crucial to the educative process.

Medical Education

"The medical profession has in recent decades made the maximum use of teaching procedures interrelating theoretical instruction and clinical experience. In the practice of an earlier day, medical classes heard learned lectures on surgery, obstetrics and dermatology, but until the years of internship had little opportunity to apply the expounded facts and principles in the ward, the operating room, or the clinic. Now, medical students, as a matter of course, *concurrently* relate theoretical instruction and actual treatment of patients. Thus students acquire a firmer and more comprehensive understanding of the principles involved and at the same time they learn the technical skills required in practice. Younger professions could profit from this experience of one of the oldest."[24]

McGrath's remarks refer to the fact that the internship no longer provides the student's first practical experience with problems of diagnosis and treatment; that function is now served by "undergraduate clinical clerkships." The failure of the internship in medicine to fulfill educational objectives is illustrative of the problems of this attempt to bridge theory and practice in other professions, including librarianship. The first publication in 1919 of the Council on Medical Education, "Essentials of an Approved Internship," designated the internship primarily "an educational experience in the course of which a certain amount of patient care might be rendered by the intern."[25] But events over the last fifty years have demonstrated that hospitals, not the educational institution, regard the student in a somewhat different role. The primacy of the educational experience gave way to the overwhelming need for reasonably skilled help gained cheaply. As Miller pointed out, "the hard fact is that an intern is more than a student; he is the source of an immensely important professional service to the institution fortunate enough to have him." Today there is a large body of opinion which holds that "the internship is an anachronism to be respected for what it once contributed but put permanently to rest."[26]

Nor do all medical educators agree with the Flexnerian model, that of a medical school wholly integrated into the university. Ebert points out that "the teaching hospital is not now, and cannot be, an integral part of the university and that attempts to force the teaching hospital into this mold are damaging both to the university and the hospital." Although little has changed in the basic organization of medical education since Flexner, "the most significant modification has been in the non-university or hospital phase of the educational process, and this change has occurred predominately in the internship-residency period of hospital training."[27]

Engineering Education

Henry Booker, a professor of engineering, perceived medical education as being unique among professions in its need to combine theory and practice in the formal schooling process. "It is interesting," he noted, "to compare the means of acquiring practical training and experience in engineering and medicine. A man intending to practice medicine obtains practical training and experience by working in teaching hospitals which are frequently located on university campuses. The procedure is highly effective and yet can be made to fit in with academic life. Doctors-in-training assist with real operations on real people. . . . There is nothing artificial about a teaching hospital. It is genuine doctoring business, and yet it can be conducted on a university campus. . . . To use a corresponding technique in engineering, it would be necessary to conduct genuine engineering business on university campuses. Real bridges would have to be designed, their erection would be supervised from university campuses, and real people would risk their necks crossing them. Imagine the howl that would go up from the local automobile dealers if, in order to provide practical experience for engineering students, the department of mechanical engineering went into a full-scale business of automobile servicing!"[28]

But this is a distorted argument. The author is personally familiar with the activities of doctoral candidates in the computer engineering program at Rensselaer Polytechnic Institute, Troy, New York, where students are encouraged if not required to engage in "real life" problems involving telecommunications, urban renewal, sewage, transportation, etc. The dissertation emphasis can be primarily theoretical or grounded in very practical experiences. Candidates include career military officers who are sent by the Armed Services to study problems that will have immediate as well as long range practical implications for defense capabilities. Furthermore, Booker's sweeping statement does not represent the consensus of engineering educators. Gordon S. Brown, among others, has presented a multiple-curriculum outline to accommodate those categories of work function that require 1) a talent for abstract thinking; 2) ability in arranging, inventing, or innovation of knowledge; 3) skill in assembling, operating and maintaining complicated machines and works; and 4) expertise in relating engineering to other technological disciplines. The choice of curriculum would depend on the proclivities of students and the needs of society.[29]

It is more accurate to say that the relative importance of theory versus practice has been a perennial issue in engineering education. Though there has been a decline in empirical methods which stress "the art and practice of engineering," there has always been   "the problem of determining the proper balance between professional education and academic (general) education. As a result a multiplicity of programs and philosophies has emerged, which has created a form of diversity that is variously viewed with delight, indifference and despair.

"Engineering education has tried, like many of the other scientifically related disciplines, to be a part of two somewhat different worlds, the professional or practitioners' world and the intellectual or academic world. . . . As a result, engineering educators find themselves divided between the pragmatic and professional demands of industry and government, on the one hand, and the theoretical and academic demands on the other hand. This represents another major problem for engineering education."[30]

Legal Education

Emphasis upon the practical aspect of legal education has received considerable impetus from leaders of the profession, including Chief Justice Burger. As U.C.L.A. Law School Dean William Warren said, "I got all the way through law school without learning what a lawyer does." As in all professional education, the pendulum swings, and for law schools the tilt is decidedly in favor of greater emphasis upon the practical aspects of legal training.

Those who applaud this trend argue that the sacred "casebook method," while it "may have developed the most discerning and sophisticated knowledge of legal principles," succeeded in graduating attorneys who remained woefully deficient in practical skills: where and how best to plead a case, how to interview clients and develop facts, how to handle settlement negotiations, and how to try the case in court. Proponents of the practical do not, of course, eschew the theoretical studies; they maintain that "both must be provided in law school because that is the only place students receive their legal training before they enter the practice of law."[31]

At the 1972 American Bar Association convention held in San Francisco, students pressed hard for "the addition of clinical education as a regular part of the curriculum, including such practical experience — particularly in helping the poor — as medical students get during their internship and residency." Student spokesmen complained that "traditional departments, which stress theory, often look down on such practical involvement." They charged that "this slants legal training in favor of corporate law and other more conservative branches of legal activities."[32]

However, not all members of the legal profession are enthusiastic about the resurgence of the practical. Lee notes that the movement "to bring prospective lawyers into closer contact with the ongoing lawyerly process" implies that students of the law have been receiving an irrelevant and second-rate education lo these many decades. But the chief benefit of law school, "the area of endeavor within which resources can be used to greatest advantage," lies not in the realm of the practical but rather the theoretical: "Since the school is a better laboratory than the practice of law in which to acquire the theoretical skills, the dominant emphasis of the law school program must continue to be in the development of those skills."[33]

Legal educators agree that the most important, widespread change in legal education "during the past decade has been the development of clinical law school courses. This teaching method gives the student an opportunity to study law from the perspective of a practitioner." But the trend is not without its problems; rather, "students in clinical courses must be closely supervised, and teachers must make themselves readily available." Scheduling difficulties have arisen. Clinical teaching materials are more expensive. And it has been "difficult to interest outstanding members of the local bar in becoming clinical instructors at law schools and even more difficult to retain them for a substantial period of time." Despite these problems, "the legitimacy and utility of these courses are no longer open to debate."[34]

Clearly, here as in other professions, arguments abound as to the appropriate mix of the practical and the theoretical in the curriculum.

Social Work Education

During the 1950s, two large studies on social work education appeared. Hollis and Taylor[35] emphasized the relationship between formal graduate education and social work practice, while criticizing the university for its failure to accept the responsibility for preparing social workers to the degree they accept it as a matter of course for the other professions. Boehm's 1959 study covers thirteen volumes of text and one index volume,[36] a comprehensive report of a curriculum study on social work education. Although Boehm's study recommends research-demonstration centers to integrate theory and practice, the traditional "practicum" has long prevailed in this field as the acceptable way to professionalize the tyro.

This acceptance has permitted social work educators to devote time to devising effective methods of resolving theoretical aims within the field learning process. But educators are still ambivalent about the amount of educational control necessary in field work. There are differing views about the nature and range of field learning opportunities, and there are conflicts over goals, concern about objectives, and dissatisfaction with existing measures for evaluating students' learning in the field.[37] Gurin's study identified two general trends in the field instruction component of social work education: 1) "a shift toward school-based and faculty-directed field instruction as against agency-based field placements," and 2) "attempts to achieve greater integration between the content of class instruction and the learning experiences in the field."[38] The former concern parallels medical education's increasing unease with the internship as a viable educational strategy.

But the relationship between the field instruction program and theoretical concerns involves structural constraints. As Cohen points out, social work educators must be responsive "not only to the formal and informal pressures of professional colleagues, agencies and associations but also to the university in its goals and aspirations." In a university, the majority of faculty are "nonprofessional-oriented academicians whose beliefs about professional education frequently reflect tolerance rather than acceptance of professional schools. . . . This is the nature of the environment in which social work educators must function to advance in acceptance, rank, and income. For them this means a concern with research, publications, theory building, and in general a negative attitude toward the development of 'vocational training' as opposed to the general problem-solving capacities thought to be the mark of the well-educated university product."[39]

This perceptive observation applies to all graduate professional education. It suggests that the very affiliation with a university obliges professional schools to emphasize theory and place a minimal value on practice. One's peers in physics or history who sit in judgment on the promotion and tenure councils do not appreciate the fact that the quality of supervision of a practicum may be equivalent in value to the publishing of three or four articles.

Teacher Education

The basis of the distinction between the classification of teacher education courses as either "theoretical" or "practical" has never been clear. The most common interpretation seems to be that "theoretical courses" are the ones with little or no outside application whereas "practical courses" are putatively useful in the real world. This interpretation has had unfortunate connotations. It suggests that theory is not practical and that what is practical is devoid of theoretical content.

Lieberman asserted that the theoretical/practical distinction should not "be used to refer to the results of courses but to the context in which they are taught."[40] Some courses, such as those in mathematics, are theoretical in the sense that they are useful in application to professional problems; however, they need not be taught in a practical context. Presumably students do not necessarily have to practice manipulative skills to grasp their context.

Virtually all programs of teacher education include both theoretical and practical courses in the above sense. Some education courses require a practical context, others do not. There are yet others which would be difficult to classify. That is, some might be improved by having the theoretical content taught in a practical context; but the need to teach them this way may not be clearly decisive, nor can the justification for the proper admixture be easily demonstrated. For these subjects, the instructor may require a few field trips or assign projects which involve some practical experience. Courses in the history and philosophy of education are manifestly theory courses, the "practical" value of which may have to await the maturity and wisdom of the student. But most courses in methods of teaching need to be taught in some practical context. Prospective teachers of high school chemistry, the argument goes, should be taught methods of teaching chemistry while they have an opportunity to observe the subject being presented to the kinds of students they will eventually teach. Their opportunities for observation and practice should not be deferred until a later time.

Student teaching at the end of the formal educational process is commonly thought to make up for the absence of a practical component in other parts of the program, and it is for this reason that most states require a period of student teaching for certification. It is by no means certain, however, that this is the most effective way to train teachers. Lieberman suggested that   " . . . the theoretical content of many education courses cannot be thoroughly understood as long as they are taught apart from demonstrations and application. Therefore, when the prospective teachers come to their period of student teaching, they have already forgotten whatever theory they may have learned in previous education courses. The effort to integrate theory and practice during student teaching fails, not because the theory is erroneous (although this is often the case) but because the students never really grasped the theory or the skills and techniques they were supposed to have learned."[41]

If a larger measure of practical training were to be included in those teacher education courses that fall logically into the theory-practice category, the prospective teacher would not have the often bewildering task of splicing together the theory that is propounded in one course and the practice in another. Deferring the student's practical experience until his or her period of student teaching eliminates most of the opportunities to discuss this experience with professors in a systematic and fruitful way. If most of the student's questions can be brought only to the supervising teacher or the director of student teaching, however sound the answers given, they may not have the theoretical perspective.

Like many other students of professional education, Lieberman uses medical education to argue his thesis. In medical education the clinical clerkship vehicle has provided practical experience in the formal program and has been seen as overcoming some of the disadvantages of the deferred internship. Lieberman urged "that we must accept substantially the same solution to the problem of integrating theory and practice in teacher education because . . . unfortunately too many programs labeled internships . . . amount to nothing more than taking some education courses simultaneously with paid (or unpaid) teaching. They reveal little or no articulation between the courses taken in the university and the school experience that would make them meaningful."[42]

But many observers cite the "absence of a deep-running" body of theory as inimical to the successful integration of theory and practice. Moreover, research on teaching has been a piecemeal affair, has been hampered by "the extreme decentralization of the basic pedagogical process," and has been hurt by a "lack of consensus about goals of instruction and the priorities among those goals." Until these critical categories are made more theoretically robust, practical applications will continue to be based on inadequate theoretical constructs.[43]

CRITERIA FOR INTEGRATING THEORY AND PRACTICE

The complexity and difficulty that inform the curricula in professional education arise from the dichotomous nature of professional work with its emphasis upon a broad theoretical foundation, and upon mastery of skills and techniques for effective practice. As occupations became professionalized by "prolonged and specialized training," responsibility for this training shifted from the historically sanctioned methods of guild and apprenticeship to an academic setting. But once there, the university insisted, by virtue of its aegis of profesional education, that the skills and techniques component of preparation be curtailed if not abandoned and the primacy of the theoretical component be asserted.

Virtually no professional school, however, has been willing to abandon elements of practical application entirely, nor has any university insisted upon a curriculum wholly devoid of experiential content. However, over the decades the disheartening aspect of argument and debate over the academic (or graduate) versus professional curriculum has been the thrust of the discussions. That is to say, the energies of educational planners have often been spent on the question of *whether* professional education should contain an experiential component rather than on the devising of the most pedagogically desirable allocation of practical endeavor within the structure of the teaching-learning process.

Hence, the often futile "theory-practice" debate. The "either-or" manner in which the proposition has been formulated has served to conceal rather than reveal the logical form of the argument. Curriculum innovation, as Heiss documented, is difficult under the clearest academic sky owing to institutional conservatism and legitimate checks and balances to curb irresponsible experimentation. It seems reasonable to accept a priori that no worthy, accredited professional school wishes to offer a curriculum consisting solely, or even largely, of "trade school" techniques, rote exercises, and routine task performances. Accordingly, the theory "as opposed to" practice argument is a false proposition, and debate on this form of the proposition is an exercise in frivolity.

Wide variation is revealed in the ways the several professional schools deal with the problem of theoretical studies and practical applications in their curricula. McGrath and others found in medical education an exemplar of successful integration of the theoretical and experiential. That this happy arrangement may reside in the very nature of the social mission of the medical arts does not, in their judgment, preclude its paradigmatic value for other professions. It can be argued that the propensity of students of professional education to measure other professional schools by what medical education does is a case of misplaced emphasis. However, with its august tradition and prestige and its highly visible goals, it does provide a convenient analogy by which to illuminate the way society prepares practitioners in the other professions.

But even if the methodology that informs medical education had no pertinence to other professions whatsoever, the problem of integrating theory and practice would remain critical to the preparation of practitioners in the several professions. Social work, teaching, nursing, journalism, and librarianship are often considered roughly on a par in terms of status of "professionalization," and in these disciplines one always finds—at the center of curriculum debate—the issue of the reconciliation of theoretical and practical concerns. The diversity of means that professions employ to educate future practitioners should not obscure a fundamental assumption shared by the majority of accredited, university-based graduate professional schools: "An ideal professional education cannot overlook the value of practical experience. . . . The question now is not the value of some practical experience but the place and extent of it in the curriculum."[44]

McGrath suggested three criteria for planning a curriculum to include the desirable allocation of practical experiences to integrate theory; in the form of questions, he asked educators to consider *What kind of experience? How much?* and *When?*

Concerning the first question, broadly stated the experience must embrace "that kind of application in which the connection between fact and theory most clearly illumines meanings previously obscured." While such a statement may be bromidic, it serves to remove experience from the fortuitous and haphazard realm criticized by Lieberman.

The next question, *How much?*, is closely related to the first. "It ought to be just enough to illuminate the principles involved and to cultivate the essential skills, but not so much as to make of learning a profitless repetitive exercise." Each learning situation differs from all the others in the complexity of the subject matter and the skills involved, and repetition may vary widely before mastery of the theoretical underpinnings is achieved. "Only enough [practice] should be required to give meaning to the theories on which practice is based and to supply the skills essential to initial employment."[45] Not only can this criterion guard against repetitious exercises of little educational value, but it may serve to define, at least generally, the parameters of the experiential component.

The third question, *When?*, relates to the temporal argument in professional education of *concurrence* or *deferment*. The latter arrangement, of which internship programs provide the commonest example, has been criticized for its potential (and actual) exploitative nature and for a failure to articulate between the experience and the educational goals of the school. The problem of adequate supervision in this context is critical; as Lieberman noted of teacher education, "It does not make sense to leave the supervision of the trainee's practical experience in the hands of persons who have less training than those who teach the theory."[46] The former procedure, which provides for interrelating theoretical instruction and clinical experience has been ably defended by McGrath and Miller in their discussions of the clinical clerkship in medical education.

To this triad a fourth consideration must be added. The question *Where?* provides a spatial reference for the other criteria. As distance from the educational setting increases, the opportunity for effective supervision decreases, and controls over the kind, quality, and extent of practice are threatened. If a resolution of theory and practice in professional education is to be achieved in a changing environment, these four questions must be continually examined and analyzed.

SUMMARY

Professional education takes place in a university milieu, a locus whose residential fee is paid in the coin of theoretical emphasis. But professional education has as its goal the pursuit of a trade, a vocation. The issue thus joined concerns the appropriate mix of the practical in an environment in which theoretical foundations are obliged to be stressed. Academic attitudes have tended to polarize around the problem of the mix, or if indeed there ought to be any manifestation of the vocational in the professional curriculum.

Shera points out that this debate lacks merit. His comments are worth quoting here, for they summarize clearly yet succinctly the false nature of the issue:

> The protracted debate over whether the professional school with its stigma of vocationalism is an interloper in the academic community has generated more emotion than substance, and in the final analysis is specious. The professional programs of study that first arose in the universities of the Middle Ages were

unblushingly vocational. The American colonial college prepared young men for the ministry, or teaching, or public service, and felt no need to apologize for its aims. Every advanced study in the academic curriculum is directed toward the preparation of the student for a career of some kind, and hence is vocational.[47]

On the other hand, few would argue that the "professional school must possess a program of study that has intellectual content, that presents a definite theoretical structure from which emerges a corpus of scholarship, and is organized in a systematic way."[48] That is, there can be no countenancing an emphasis upon the trivial aspects of professional practice or a disdain of intellectual activity. In a realistic fashion, the question to be argued is: What is the proper amount of the practical component in professional education?

While rational discussion of the balance of theory and practice in the curricula of professional schools acknowledges that both components are desirable, arguments yet abound concerning the kinds of practical experiences, their temporal and spatial characteristics, and the quantity or degree of the training. A brief survey of medical, engineering, legal, social work, and teacher education reveals a vigorous if often frustrating examination of the problem of reconciling theory and practice. The criteria McGrath suggested will serve our study as we explore the manifold possibilities of integrating education and experience within the structure of traditional and experimental teaching-learning processes.

Paths to be explored in the ensuing chapters will seek answers to difficult questions of theory and practice, methods of instruction best suited to integrate knowledge and experience, and the nature of the teaching-learning process itself. The historical record will indicate that there are, indeed, no sure or easy solutions. As Holley noted, "Any practitioner discipline has a difficult time relating theory to practice. Shall we teach '*how* to do it' or '*why* we do it'? . . . What usually happens when we raise such questions is that we seek a form of accommodation with some theory and some practice."[49] But accommodation must be grounded in sound pedagogy and practical wisdom. That professional education is most effective in which "direct participation in the daily business of teaching and learning can be joined to systematic study of tested practice based on continuing inquiry and appraisal."[50]

REFERENCES

[1]William J. McGlothlin, "Insights from One Profession Which May Be Applied to Educating for Other Professions," *Current Issues in Higher Education* (proceedings of the 16th Annual National Conference on Higher Education), ed. G. Kerry Smith (Washington, D.C.: Association for Higher Education, 1961), p. 120.

[2]Lloyd E. Blauch (ed.), *Education for the Professions* (Washington: GPO, 1955), p. 9.

[3]Abraham Flexner, *Medical Education in the United States and Canada* (Boston: Merrymount Press, 1910).

[4]Abraham Flexner, "Is Social Work a Profession?," *Proceedings of the National Conference of Charities and Corrections* (Chicago: Hildmann Printing Company, 1915), pp. 576-90.

[5]A. M. Carr-Saunders and P. A. Wilson, *The Professions* (Oxford: Clarendon Press, 1933), p. 491.

[6]T. R. McConnell et al., "The University and Professional Education," *Education for the Professions*, Sixty-first Yearbook of the National Society for the Study of Education, Part II, ed. Nelson B. Henry (Chicago: University of Chicago Press, 1962), p. 359.

[7]Robert M. Hutchins, *The University of Utopia* (Chicago: University of Chicago Press, 1953), p. 40.

[8]J. A. Bartky, "The School of Education and the University," *Journal of Higher Education*, XXVI (May, 1955), 256.

[9]McConnell et al., loc. cit.

[10]Ibid., p. 260.

[11]Blauch (ed.), op. cit., passim.

[12]Ibid., p. 9.

[13]McGlothlin, op. cit., p. 121.

[14]Bernard Berelson, *Graduate Education in the United States* (New York: McGraw-Hill, 1960), p. 223.

[15]McConnell et al., op. cit., p. 260.

[16]Ann M. Heiss, *Challenges to Graduate Schools* (San Francisco: Josey-Bass, 1970), p. 243.

[17]McConnell et al., loc. cit.

[18]John G. Darley, "The Graduate School As a Professional School," *Education for the Professions*, Sixty-first Yearbook of the National Society for the Study of Education, Part II, ed. Nelson B. Henry (Chicago: University of Chicago Press, 1962), p. 207.

[19]Lester G. Anderson, "Professional Education: Present Status and Continuing Problems," *Education for the Professions*, Sixty-first Yearbook of the National Society for the Study of Education, Part II, ed. Nelson B. Henry (Chicago: University of Chicago Press, 1962), p. 18.

[20]Ibid.

[21]McGlothlin, loc. cit.

22Earl J. McGrath, "The Ideal Education for the Professional Man," *Education for the Professions*, Sixty-first Yearbook of the National Society for the Study of Education, Part II, ed. Nelson B. Henry (Chicago: University of Chicago Press, 1962), p. 290.

23McGlothlin, op. cit., p. 122.

24McGrath, loc. cit.

25Council on Medical Education, American Medical Association, *The Graduate Education of Physicians: A Report of the Citizens Commission on Graduate Medical Education* (Chicago: The Association, 1966), p. 13.

26George E. Miller, "Medicine," *Education for the Professions*, Sixty-first Yearbook of the National Society for the Study of Education, Part II, ed. Nelson B. Henry (Chicago: University of Chicago Press, 1962), p. 112.

27Robert H. Ebert, "Medical Education in the United States," *Daedalus*, 106 (Winter, 1977), 183, 171.

28Henry G. Booker, Letters, *Science*, 141 (August 9, 1963), 486, 488.

29Gordon S. Brown, "Modern Education in Science and Technology: Pace Setter of Industrial Technology" (Paper Presented at the Long-range Planning Conference, Trends to 1975), October 21-23, 1964, Palo Alto, California, Stanford Research Institute. (Mimeographed).

30William K. LeBold, et al., "Reactions to the Preliminary Report of the Goals Study," *Journal of Engineering Education*, 57 (1967), 438.

31Richard L. Braun, "Practical Skills in the Law School Curriculum," *University of Dayton Law Review*, 2 (1977), 12.

32*New York Times*, August 20, 1972, Section 4, p. 7.

33Rex E. Lee, "Theory and Practice in Training for the Law: Thinking Like a Lawyer and Doing What He Does," *University of Dayton Law Review*, 2 (1977), 3, 6.

34Sherman G. Finesilver, "The Tension between Practical and Theoretical Legal Education: A Judge's View of the Gap," *Brigham Young University Law Review*, 3 (1977), 1062-63.

35Ernest V. Hollis and Alice L. Taylor, *Social Work Education in the United States* (New York: Columbia University Press, 1951).

36Werner W. Boehm (dir.), *Social Work Curriculum Study* (New York: Council on Social Work Education, 1959).

37Council on Social Work Education, *Field Learning and Teaching: Explorations in Graduate Social Work Education* (Proceedings of the Symposium Working Party on Field Learning and Teaching, October 29-November 1, 1967, New Orleans) (New York: The Council, 1968), pp. 4-5.

[38]Arnold Gurin, *Community Organization Curriculum in Graduate Social Work Education: Report and Recommendations* (New York: Council on Social Work Education, 1970), p. 20.

[39]Jerome Cohen, "Selected Constraints in the Relationship between Social Work Education and Practice," *Journal of Education for Social Work*, 13 (Winter, 1977), 5-6.

[40]Myron Lieberman, *The Future of Public Education* (Chicago: University of Chicago Press, 1960), p. 113.

[41]Ibid., p. 114.

[42]Ibid., p. 118.

[43]Harold E. Mitzel, "Increasing the Impact of Theory and Research on Programs of Instruction," *Journal of Teacher Education*, 28 (November-December, 1977), 17.

[44]McGrath, loc. cit.

[45]Ibid., pp. 290-91.

[46]Lieberman, op. cit., p. 117.

[47]Jesse H. Shera, *The Foundations of Education for Librarianship* (New York: John Wiley & Sons, Inc., 1972), p. 346.

[48]Ibid., p. 347.

[49]Edward G. Holley, "Library Education and the Library Profession," *Texas Library Journal*, 53 (Spring, 1977), 75.

[50]Lawrence A. Cremin, "The Education of the Educating Professions," *Research Bulletin: Horace Mann-Lincoln Institute*, 18 (March, 1978), 7.

2

LIBRARY EDUCATION

INTRODUCTION

It is not surprising to find in library education problems similar to those found in education for the other professions. As professional schools have become members of the university family, they have been obliged to demonstrate their fealty to the parent by emphasizing the theoretical component of instruction, usually to the neglect or downgrading of the experiential component. Like other professions, the claims of librarianship as a university discipline have been validated in this way.

But if the dominant characteristics of professional education in earlier times were academic and theoretical, there has appeared in recent years a compensatory effort "to restore the human being as the chief focus of professional concerns" and "a renewed interest in clinical or field experience."[1] Chapter 1 noted examples of this trend in selected professional schools. Mayhew articulated the current emphasis by noting that "the one pervasive reform is the attempt in most professional schools to increase clinical or field experience and to initiate it much earlier in students' education."[2] That this development has been decried by those who fear an intellectual debasement of the curriculum does not negate its importance.

Current trends in graduate professional education appear to signal a reexamination of and an emphasis on the clinical or field aspect of training. Library education may be examined as a specific case of the general state of professional education, for the problems of graduate training in a university setting and the pull and tug of theory and practice in the curriculum influence librarianship in the same manner as that perceived by other professional disciplines.

But a number of library educators aver that schools remain indifferent or opposed to all the manifold possibilities inherent in the practical component. If, in Rothstein's phrase, the current skepticism as to the value of work contacts in the curriculum of library schools "derives from history rather than logic,"[3] a review of that history ought to shed some light upon current attitudes and practices.

THE LIBRARY SCHOOL AND THE
UNIVERSITY ENVIRONMENT

When Melvil Dewey decided to establish, in 1887, the School of Library Economy at Columbia University, his chief detractors argued against its necessity. William F. Poole, for example, felt that "practical work in a library, based on a good previous education in the schools, was the only proper way to train good librarians."[4] Other eminent colleagues in the field at that time, like Justin Winsor and John Shaw Billings, contended emphatically against Dewey's proposal to create a school to teach librarianship.

On the other hand, the trustees of Columbia were primarily upset at Dewey's decision to admit women to the program. Dewey disobeyed their orders, admitted women to the school, and for his disobedience was subsequently forced to resign as Columbia's librarian. In 1889 he moved to Albany to become New York State librarian, took the school with him, and established it as the New York State library school. In 1926, the Albany school was reinstated at Columbia and combined with the Library School of the New York Public Library. Dewey himself had long since retired from the library profession, but by this time formal library education was established in a university setting.

The establishment was rather more geographical than prestigious; but it is noteworthy that early objections, both from the field and from the university, had nothing to do with arguments about the intellectual worth of the training. It is well known that early formal library education was heavily weighted on the practical side. The baldly stated curricular purpose of the School of Library Economy in 1886-87 would be embarrassing even to the most vocationally oriented of present day community colleges. Dewey's training emphasized achieving perfection in technical details, thus enabling graduates to step directly into positions of administration and management.[5] Programs of this nature superficially resembled an apprenticeship, but due to systematic instruction, they "afforded the student an opportunity of mastering in a minimum of time the various subjects embraced in the curriculum and of seeing them through an over-all and unified perspective impossible through apprenticeship in a single library."[6] It is well to remember that the time-saving factor has always been a legitimate justification for professional training of a formal kind over solely an on-the-job learning experience.

The several library schools, many of them founded by Dewey's early students, existed in the university ambience under what appears in retrospect as the apathy of benign neglect until the Williamson report of 1923. Charles C. Williamson, then librarian of the Municipal Reference Library in New York City, was appointed to undertake an investigation of the status of library training. Out of his studies, conducted from 1919 to 1921, a work entitled *Training for Library Service*[7] was published. Destined to become the single most influential document in the history of American library education, the report became, for librarianship, the homologue of Abraham Flexner's monumental 1910 study of medical education.[8]

The Williamson report focused attention on the low quality of library education in the United States and offered numerous recommendations to correct weaknesses and upgrade the quality of training. To do this, Williamson knew that Dewey's essentially clerical approach had to be recognized for what it was. The difference between the two general types of library work that Williamson observed, professional and clerical, had "not been kept clearly in view in library organization and administration, and they therefore tend to be confused in the work of the library schools." In its author's own view, and presciently as events transpired, "one of the most important conclusions of this study is that the professional library school should be organized as a department of a university, along with other professional schools, rather than in public libraries, state or municipal."[9] Only six of the fifteen so-called professional schools investigated by Williamson had a university connection; the rest were affiliated with public or state libraries.

The machinery of accreditation followed shortly after the Williamson study. The gradual yet steady "professionalization" of library education from Williamson to 1960 has been thoroughly documented by the research of Churchwell[10] and Carroll,[11] and training antecedent to the famous report has been studied by Vann.[12] If Williamson saw graduate school status as the chief way, in Wilson's words, "to jar the profession out of its prolonged devotion to the practical techniques set up by Dewey,"[13] it did not insure intellectual respectability as a matter of course. Carroll pointed out that the terms "professional study" and "graduate education" were seen as *qualitatively* different: "The former was thought to involve the transmission of knowledge necessary for the beginning practitioner in his first job. The latter involved the creation of knowledge comparable with the graduate schools of other professions, as preparation for scholarly and highly specialized work and for administrative and executive positions."[14]

Concerning library education at the graduate level, Carroll observed the same terminological confusion that Blauch and Berelson discerned in professional education:[15] "After the 1951 *Standards for Accreditation*, library schools generally changed their names to graduate library schools and the first degree was generally regarded as a graduate degree. However, it could more accurately be defined as a graduate-professional degree, leaving the terms graduate degree and graduate study to be used to describe degrees and study beyond the initial preparation for librarianship."[16]

Following the reaccreditation programs of 1953-1957, the term graduate education "could be applied to all accredited library school programs." But this is not to argue, Carroll noted, "that instruction in all of the . . . schools was of the same caliber, or that the merely technical and professional aspects of the librarian's education had been eliminated and replaced by a completely theoretical curriculum such as is sometimes envisioned when one speaks of graduate study. In fact, it would appear that the distinction between graduate study and professional education has never been clear and is particularly liable to confusion in the professional schools."[17]

What does seem clear is that the sort of trivial, routinized library education that Williamson censured in his report does not exist, save in homeopathic doses, in accredited, graduate schools of librarianship. At the same time, "methods of acquiring knowledge relevant to solving the problems of librarianship,"[18] in Harlow's phrase, does not preclude a consideration of the many diverse, creative ways to prepare the candidates for the immediate as well as the distant future.

THEORY AND PRACTICE IN LIBRARY EDUCATION

In 1960 Carnovsky summarized a representative sampling of criticisms of library education. That the sample is widely divergent and contradictory attests to a plethora of unshared perceptions of the objectives of library training. Programs were criticized as being "too theoretical; too much emphasis is placed on principles and theory and not enough on the realities of library practice." Another complaint found training to be "too detailed, emphasizing trivial matters that are readily mastered on the job or that are merely obvious; more attention should be paid to theory and basic principles." Other criticisms scored the poor quality of teaching, "pitched at a level considerably below that of graduate study" and courses that were "padded and repetitious." Specifically, the course in library administration was singled out for censure; it "too often neglects consideration of real library problems. As now given in some library schools, it is a waste of time."[19]

It can be argued with considerable justice that a composite report of this kind shows merely that some schools are doing different things, or that students' perceptions of "real library problems" are often notoriously unrealistic. But a laundry list of complaints like this does show a degree of disaffection with the content and methodology of library education. In the instances where programs were adjudged too theoretical, for example, some validity in that observation likely obtains. Swank pointed out that "a great deal of earnest effort in recent years has gone into the teaching of the theoretical foundations of librarianship as against the unilluminated practice of it."[20] By the same token, any but the most unsophisticated student can sense those elements in the curriculum that are patently trivial in nature. The range of complaints indicated a commonality with other professional education in its absence of a perceived balance of the theoretical and the practical.

Williamson

In the deserved praise and attention given to the Williamson report for providing the great stimulus to library education, often overlooked are the closely reasoned arguments about the nature and scope of practice work in the curriculum. Williamson acknowledged that "skill in the performance of any kind of library work must be wrought out by actually doing the work" and accepted the place of practical application in complementing formal classroom studies. "Every library school," he noted, "recognizes to some extent the desirability of supplementing its theoretical instruction by contact with or active participation in some kind of actual library work." What he decried was a pervasive lack of "understanding of the underlying pedagogical principles involved."

First, a clear understanding of principles was obscured by the hazy terminology then employed. "Practical work" as distinguished from "practice work" had been used often to refer to experiences in actual library conditions which were a priori perceived as having educational value. In some cases "practical work" was supervised by the school; in other cases supervision was remote or altogether lacking. "Practice work" was the proper term to define "work done by the student either in preparation for or following and definitely related to the class-room exercises." "Field work," another term Williamson found to be used vaguely, had in some schools the same meaning as "practical work," an experience often removed from the control and educational purposes of the school. One school, Wisconsin, used the terms "practice," "field practice," and "practical work" interchangeably. "Certain schools used the term 'laboratory work' with the idea, apparently, that such a simile tends to put their field work on a more scientific basis or on a little higher plane," the author remarked wryly.

Second, Williamson could find no rational explanation for the length of time allotted to the several experiences that supplemented formal classroom work: "The amount of field work included in the one-year library school course would seem to have no scientifically determined basis."[21] To McGrath's question, *How much?* and McGlothlin's concern over any rationale behind the various work-related experiences in professional education generally, Williamson found "practical work" in the schools ranging from four weeks of the term to "three hundred and forty-eight hours scattered throughout [the] year, with two weeks 'blocked practice' in February."[22]

Such variation, Williamson noted, arose in part because schools differed in their opinions as to the relative merit of providing deferred practice after theory or concurrent experience with theory. But the author found no instances in which the schools attempted to verify the better method by "careful experimentation or scientific procedure. It seems very doubtful whether it can ever be possible for any school to arrange schedules of instruction in such a manner that students will actually have their practical and theoretical work on every subject at the same time."[23]

A final major defect in the proper educational management of what Williamson analyzed under the rubric "Field Work" concerned the kinds of assignments given to students. Frequently he found "no clear-cut and well-defined objective." No thought was given to student needs or interests; more importantly, no thought was given as to *why* needs and interests, skills already demonstrated and skills in need of a reality base, or principles to be learned and tasks to be performed *should* be conceptualized in pedagogical terms.

Williamson issued a warning which, when unheeded, has remained a source of trouble in the administration of field projects or internships to this day. Addressing the sanguine claims of institutions, proud of the fact that their "students are sent into libraries to work as members of the staff under *actual* library conditions," he took exception to the assumed value of this approach: "Actual library work is not carried on for the benefit of the staff or to give instruction to students." Admittedly, interns would inevitably absorb some knowledge and principles, but that would be "purely incidental to a vast amount of routine work; and some very intelligent people work all their lives in a good library without getting a professional outlook."[24]

Reminiscent of the arguments in medical education that have now led to a reshaping of the hospital internship, Williamson found that "student practice is in general poorly supervised and inadequately analyzed and reported to the school." Few librarians have the time to guide competently a novice under the pressures of actual conditions. The student, moreover, does not have an "opportunity to observe minutely, critically, and comparatively" the operations of the institution. At worst, the situation results in exploitation, at best "a waste of time."

Williamson discovered in library training what Lieberman and others observed for teacher education: "The present system of field practice does not sufficiently clinch and check up theories learned from lectures and reading." In a perceptive statement he summarized the problem and suggested principles which have been often overlooked or neglected by library educators for over half a century:

> The fundamental purpose of field experience should determine the method of making assignments. If the purpose is to acquire skill, then future work and present interests should be the determining factor. If grasp of principles and better understanding of subjects taught is the purpose, then the practical work, if it cannot cover all subjects, should be selected to represent the branches in which the student has not shown proficiency. . . . If the aim is to try him out, to see whether his success in actual work is what could be anticipated from class-room work, then

the type of field work does not greatly matter, and nearly everything depends on the skill of the supervisor and the kind of report made to the school officials.

It seems clear from his report that Williamson was concerned with the educational soundness of practical work in the curriculum, not with the argument over whether a professional education should or should not have a practical component. He correctly insisted that McGrath's questions of *What kind of experience?*, *How much?*, and *When?*, and the question, *Where?*, be justified within a conceptual framework of pedagogical objectives. He found that failure to heed these critical aspects of trainng, in the schools he analyzed, resulted in their lack of any conscious philosophy.[25]

Reece

After Williamson, no better analysis of the manifold problems in creating a sound curriculum for library education can be found than that prepared by Ernest J. Reece. His study, *The Curriculum in Library Schools*, was published in 1936 as Volume IV in the Columbia University Studies in Library Service, for which Williamson was chairman of the editorial committee. The author's official title was Melvil Dewey Professor of Library Service at Columbia University.

Like Williamson, Reece rejected a priori the argument whether there ought to be an experiential component in library education: "If there is one thing upon which all persons concerned with professional education must agree it is that participation in actual work is antecedent to competence and therefore an indispensable factor in the preparation of novitiates." Moreover, he accepted as established principle that "certain learning processes go forward only under conditions involving action. . . . This holds alike for routines and for tasks which entail complicated mental reactions."[26]

Going beyond Williamson's analysis of practical supplements to the curriculum, Reece constructed a classification of what he broadly called "work contacts." His taxonomy divided these contacts into six "forms" which may be summarized as follows:

Class Presentation: In law and business schools takes the form of the case method of teaching; in medical education, amphitheater surgery; in dental education, demonstration of ceramic processes and effects.

Laboratory Work: Involves operations carefully prescribed and performed under direction of an instructor in a course. In law schools takes the form of moot courts organized in course; in applied sciences by exercises in laboratory.

Problems: Essentially unsupervised course work; takes the form of independent assignments, or assigned work where student assumes responsibility for organization and completion; exemplified in schools of architecture by the *projet*.

Projects: Takes the form of participative clinical activity in hospitals for medical education; managed most advantageously if built into a course; characterized by concurrent rather than deferred activities; entails "the problematic act carried to completion in its natural setting."

Observation: Exemplified in architecture by inspection of buildings; in engineering by visits to plants; in schools of education by watching classes in session; preferably to be organized as a course or part of a course.

Field Work: Assumes the form of alternating work and study scheduling; in medical education by internship; relative to the other forms, detachment from the school and interpreting entire curriculum rather than a course.[27]

Reece argued that these categories of the practical component hold for library education, though the library schools "have made intelligent discussion and treatment of work contacts difficult for themselves by glossing the above distinctions and by loose use of terms." Class presentations include processes (book repairing) and use of the case method (principles of administration and book selection "through the instancing of actual or hypothecated situations"). Laboratory work, "although lacking the discovery element," enjoys wide acceptance by teachers of cataloging. Problems have been "the staple and indispensable method of instruction in reference work and bibliography." Projects include "the organizing of book collections . . . and the planning and execution of programs for institutes" (that is, a study of user needs in a defined demographic area, or circulation problems in an academic library). Observation includes visits to types of libraries, inspection of a classed catalog, or "the journey to a system or series of libraries by an entire school." Finally, field work "has been a natural inheritance from the days of training under preceptors, and its unquestioned value has assured its persistence . . . to the present time."

But it is precisely this "unquestioned value" of field work that exercised Reece's critical faculties, as it did Williamson's. If one contrasts the first five categories, or "forms," with field work, one notices a singular difference. Whereas practical exercises, whatever their variety and scope, are fundamentally course-controlled, field work perforce lies without rather than within the formal curriculum. Order, control and conservation of time were, for Reece, the raisons d'être of professional preparation. To the extent that field work necessarily precluded these elements of formal training, they became difficult to justify on theoretical grounds.

Echoing Williamson's findings, Reece cited a 1925 report by the Committee on Field Work of the Association of American Library Schools which demonstrated that "library schools predominately have scattered their field-work assignments in bits throughout the weeks and days of the school year; or have interrupted class activities to provide for them in blocked form, often abbreviating thereby the periods available for study in course and perhaps ignoring differences among forms of instruction." Even allowing for intrinsic virtues in field work, the report indicated that its very form logically contravenes the instructional program.

Reece analyzed the salient qualities of field work, as they existed in his day. Field work is not limited to one section of the curriculum or to one subject; there is the possibility (but not the inevitability) of holistic learning by the participant. It seeks to give "conversance and facility in the life situation." And it is most efficacious when most shaped by unpredictability; "necessarily, therefore, to plan it meticulously and to methodize it thoroughly would be prejudicial." In this set of values Reece observed a common feature: the lack of control over the teaching-learning process, no matter how carefully field-work assignments were constructed. In the certainty of unpredictability Reece found his major conceptual objection.

Recognizing that librarians have taken pride in the "teaching function" of their work, he did not want the reader to infer "that instruction approaching in effectiveness that of the classroom is impossible in a library and at the hands of librarians." But his list of conditions under which successful teaching could take place leaves no doubt that a confluence of such conditions would be not only rare but "to most intents and purposes nonexistent." The arguments against field work are essentially those Williamson noted; key words and phrases reappear, such as "faulty planning," "carelessly directed," "waste of time," "student exploitation." Librarians in institutions where field work occurs hold appointment "by reason of fitness for library work, not because of ability to teach." Though he acquiesced in the continuance of field work in library school programs as inevitable, he was vocal in insisting that it be somehow separated from the curriculum, preferably in summer blocks or postschool service.[28]

From Reece to the Present

Following Reece's cogent statements there have been a number of articles, monographs, and addresses by librarians and library educators concerning the practical component in curriculum planning. For various reasons the later proponents of some kind of well planned, systematic effort to supplement classroom theory have been arguing a minority viewpoint. There voices, largely unheeded, were muted for reasons advanced in the preceding analysis of the conflicting priorities in professional education. Institutional difficulties have been cited as impeding efforts to construct a viable program of practice work, though these did not hinder the medical field. Of perhaps more importance is the pejorative connotation of "practical" work in a university ostensibly devoted to the pursuit of theory. The ancient gnome of the university being "in society but not of society" undoubtedly renders suspect attempts to inject into the curriculum too heady a dosage of "real life" experience. Finally, and this may be the most legitimate objection, many experiments in devising suitable experiences to illuminate theory have been ill conceived. The warnings of Williamson and Reece of the imperative need to ground work contacts on legitimate pedagogical principles have largely been ignored. This nexus of conflicting pressures caused Rothstein to remark, concerning field work, that for most schools of librarianship the game was not worth the candle.[29]

Francis R. St. John's study of internship for librarians was undertaken at the request of the Board of Education for Librarianship of the American Library Association in January, 1937, and his analysis was published in 1938, two years after the Reece report.

At the outset, St. John assumed as given the superior merit of the internship over the apprenticeship. The latter he defined as "learning in service without previous theoretical training" and noted that this was the predominate means of entry into the library profession in Europe. The former was defined as "supervised, planned training which allows the application of full theoretical training to actual, varied practice." Following a useful review of selected internship programs in other professions, St. John assayed a defense of the internship in the form of questions and answers to eleven problems he deemed crucial to effective planning of such programs.[30]

Rejecting a period of training before beginning library school on the grounds that practice cannot precede theory, St. John opted for a period of training after course work is completed but before a degree or certificate is granted. Insisting that the responsibility for the training "rest directly with the library school," he admitted that "this system of training would be difficult to supervise because there are not enough libraries in the immediate vicinity of most library schools to permit adequate supervised training of all students."

How does one overcome this difficulty? If reports of teachers are combined with reports of the supervising librarians, "it would be possible to get a fairly complete picture of the student both in school and under actual working conditions." Monthly progress reports plus "friendly and informal chats or luncheons with a faculty adviser" ought to insure that the intern is usefully applying the theory he learned in class to the actual work situation. Of course this method is time-honored in more formal teacher-student relationships in graduate study, like certain seminars, independent study, and doctoral guidance for oral and written examinations and for the thesis. But such casual liaison as an educational desideratum has never been satisfactorily demonstrated.

As to the nature of experiences considered useful, St. John argued for an arrangement in which "the student may specialize in the particular kind of library work which interests him most." But this assumes at all times a happy correspondence of individual desires and institutional needs; unfortunately, it does not necessarily allow for experiences which would integrate theory and practice. Much of established library work is routinized; the paradox is that the more highly structured and smoothly operating the institution is, the more habitual the work experience becomes. Hence, an educational experience, a true "learning" situation, may be least well-served in the so-called better libraries.

Concerning the length of time for the internship, St. John recommended that "prospective executives or leaders should have a more intensive training than other graduates." Equating intensity with length, the author placed the time period at from six months to a year.   "Knowledge of a particular job does not seem to be the goal of internships, however. A picture of the entire field, with all work undertaken viewed as part of the whole, is much more important."[31]

The author touched upon other salient matters, such as cost, supervision by the American Library Association, pilot programs, and the like. The subsequent kudos for St. John's report must be tempered by measuring its proposals against the Williamson and Reece studies and against the general thesis developed in the preceding pages. St. John's comments on the molar approach to internship training are consistent with that aspect of field work judged worthwhile by Williamson and Reece. But St. John made no suggestion to resolve the dilemma of lack of proper supervision by the school and responsibility of the school for the interns. Nor are the evaluative capabilities of casual, informal feedback educationally sound. The presumed convergence of interest with institution ignores both institutional need and the residue of unilluminated theory the student may carry from classroom to practice. Finally, Reece's concerns over control and over the fundamental exclusivity of teaching function and competence as a practitioner go unanswered.

The respective roles to be allocated practice and theory continued as an important facet of discussion in the counsels of library education in the 1940s.[32] Danton's 1946 monograph on library education provided a useful summary of the dilemmas inherent in the expectations of employers and the quality of preparation in a graduate institution affiliated with a university. While Danton's report was not concerned with the problems of field work or internship specifically, his general indictment was central to the theoretical-practical argument: overemphasis on techniques "has probably been the most recurrent and generally agreed-upon criticism of the library schools for the past quarter of a century or more."[33] That the library schools were not wholly to blame for this emphasis is suggested by the pressures of practitioners who insisted upon a certain demonstrable skill in techniques when the tyro reported for his first position. But this implied, in

Goldhor's phrase, "a subservient relationship of the training agencies of the profession to the practitioners"[34] not to be found in other more prestigious professions.

Of course, employers want both skilled technicians and personnel "trained in courses which emphasize the theoretical and philosophical aspects of librarianship," but Danton saw this as unrealistic given the current programs as they were constituted. Moreover, the profession did not differentiate between clerical and professional activities. Library schools, following rather than leading the profession, failed in many cases to provide that distinction to students. Consequently, the self-fulfilling prophecy perpetuated itself. It is useful to recall here that Reece never suggested, in his taxonomy, that the forms of practice work within classroom control and supervision be of the sort that "any high school graduate with two months of indoctrination could do equally well."

Danton's recommendations to reduce the "non-professional content of the librarian's education" and upgrade the academic level of instruction provided for an "intensified core curriculum devoted to the whys and wherefores of major library methods and techniques" to precede advanced study.[35] This was, presumably, the proper locus for whatever practical work was considered necessary to illuminate theory. The very necessity of Danton's report is unfortunate testimony to the relative absence of change that had taken place in the two and a half decades since Williamson.

Other library educators during this period shared Danton's concern that library education be truly graduate education. Metcalf noted that "at present a considerable part of the instruction in library schools is still of a purely clerical type and makes no demands on the superior abilities of the graduate student." Allowing that some learning of this kind "may be inherent in the necessary preparation for librarianship," he relegated this component to a minor role in the curriculum. Mature students, he believed, "either will be familiar with [techniques] already or can quickly pick them up after being introduced to the basic principles that underlie the clerical phases of the library routine."[36]

The case for an even sharper separation of the theoretical and the practical than Danton's critique implied was urged by Lancour. Advances in librarianship have been made in precisely those areas where "library education has been subjected to the critical appraisal of library educators and not librarians." Too much practical experience is a hindrance, not an aid, to those whose task it is to prepare the student for a changing profession: "I would far rather that the student be stimulated by concepts and ideas which may at the moment be quite impractical than to have him lose the ideas which may be commonplace ten years hence."[37]

But if theory is permitted to override all other considerations in the curriculum, the pendulum will have swung too far in the other direction. Wheeler tempered the dominant thrust of the educators in the 1940s by iterating the need for a judicious balance between theoretical considerations and the processes of technique. Quoting a scientist's observation that "nine-tenths of every program of scientific research consists of routine drudgery, almost devoid of any intellectual element," Wheeler claimed that too many in the profession disdain routines and details. A perennial argument is again raised here: How can professionals train clerical workers in routines if they themselves are ignorant of process? But the educational question is whether this should be a function of the profession or of library schools. At the time Wheeler waxed pessimistic, doubting that this conflict could be resolved.[38]

While the theory-practice dilemma was being argued with respect to classroom content as the central consideration in this period, extramural activities as a function of the curriculum were by no means ignored. Metcalf et al. attempted to set forth what ideally an internship should accomplish: "If a student, in addition to taking a first year of library school, spends a further year in various parts of a well-organized and well-administered library, he will be in a position, through observation and through contact with competent librarians, to master both the practical and the theoretical sides of library work." The important elements in the success of such a program are 1) that the student be given the opportunity to observe and to reason for himself, and 2) that responsible staff members be given the time to instruct the intern in the governing principles of the library's administration and organization.[39]

Field work, as distinguished from internship, involved for Metcalf "practice work" in a neighboring library. Metcalf and his colleagues were quick to point out that since this is usually carried out under the supervision of "librarians unconnected with the library school," no credit should be assigned to this experience. Furthermore, "the chief difficulty with this system is that the student has no one to supervise his work critically or from a theoretical point of view." The value of field work is "likely to be in proportion to the degree of supervision that is exercised by the teaching staff." The authors indicated that this experience, to be most profitable, ought to be given "shortly after the student has mastered the most important theoretical concepts related to library science."[40] Implicit in Metcalf's discussion of both types of extramural elements was that internships are to be supervised and should involve both theory and techniques, whereas field work is likely to be poorly supervised and consist primarily of routine chores.

Virtually alone among library educators in his efforts to reopen the case for field work as a viable pedagogical element of the curriculum during this period was Neil Van Deusen. Unlike Reece, who did not distinguish between "field work" and "internship" in his forms of work contacts, Van Deusen defined field work as school-initiated agreements with various types of libraries for student practice, usually in blocked periods during the formal course of study.

Van Deusen discovered, by surveying the thirty-four then-accredited library schools, that the twin assaults of Williamson and Reece on the educational shortcomings of field work had affected library training significantly. But he also found that, although field work requirements had declined since 1923, a majority of educators still considered the experience "invaluable." To explain this paradox, Van Deusen analyzed the responses to his survey and found three categories of educational value that were repudiated by the Williamson and Reece reports: 1) Field work was "a teaching device which clinches classroom points, reveals interrelationship of courses, and makes the textbooks come alive"; 2) field work "develops student confidence and poise, and increases professional enthusiasm"; and 3) field work, in small "one-man" situations, acquaints students (especially those entering the field of school librarianship) with "the variety of practical problems for which they will be responsible."

Van Deusen saw the objections to field work as being not intrinsically educational but rather a problem of inadequate funds, time and effort. Only technological difficulties stand in the way of a situation in which field work would be ideal. For Van Deusen the basic question of a philosophy of librarianship was somewhat Skinnerian: a problem of refining specific techniques, a fitting of elements rather than an exploration of the nature of the elements themselves: "The crucial problems in a philosophy of librarianship are not scientific or philosophical, but engineering problems concerned with time, money and personnel with ingenuity for fitting means to ends."[41]

In looking to the decade of the 1950s to discern new patterns that might be emerging, Leigh found no observable trend for the increase or decrease of "the part played by practice work, laboratory or clinical work, and organized observation in the library education curriculum." He found this stasis "surprising in consideration of the thought, effort, and experiment, which some of the other professions, new and old, have devoted to this kind of training."[42] Dominant was the view that the practical element had become somewhat of an embarrassment to professional status and stature in library education. The theoreticians had been apotheosized into educators "who have not been repressed by the defeatism of the field worker."[43] Despite a cavalier air, however, the Dean of the Division of the Social Sciences of Chicago University, in addressing a group of library educators in 1948, listed as a major problem in all professions "the inadequate connection between theory and practice" and cited general neglect in coming to grips with the relationship between the two.[44]

This absence of enthusiasm in seeking ways of resolving the theory-practice conundrum is evidenced by the relative infrequency in the literature on the topic. Despite Leigh's statement that the major unsolved problem in education for librarianship was "how to achieve balance in the basic professional year between theoretical training and the learning of practical techniques,"[45] the energies of library educators lay elsewhere.

A notable exception to the silence was Stallmann's 1954 review of library internships. Noting that little had been written on internship programs since the St. John study, she took cognizance of the generally misunderstood nature of this practical element with the resulting attribution to it of diverse and contradictory purposes. Citing the usual problems of nomenclature that have inhibited clarity of thought in this area, Stallmann offered a definition from teacher education which suggested the relationship of theory to practice in broad connotation: "a phase of professional education in which a student works for a period of time in the field in order to develop a capacity to carry professional responsibilities."[46]

After briefly but usefully reviewing internship methods in medicine, dietetics, clinical psychology, social work, and public administration, Stallmann argued that library internships provide an excellent vehicle with which "to build a closer and more appropriate connection between theory and practice." Like Van Deusen, she saw the potential problem of the internship as a matter of developing clear objectives. In many cases sloppy administration and poor coordination between the library school and the participating institution had vitiated the educational value of the program. But beyond that, she admitted that "without the right kind of student and without the happiest selection of library and staff, the internship will not be as rewarding as it should be regardless of the trappings and red tape that may surround it." The problem, of course, with such a fortuitous abstraction is that it can be called upon to serve as an argument for its opposite. It is as theoretically possible to conceive of another system, or no system at all, to effect connection between theory and practice given the right student and the "happiest selection" of supervision and institution.

Nevertheless, Stallmann presented a reasonably detailed and specific plan for an internship program. It involved a report or thesis to be written by the student based upon his intern experience. The student would commence the internship period at the end of his formal library school studies, but graduation from the school would be contingent upon successful completion of the program and defense of the thesis. Length of service was to be a minimum of six months and a maximum of eleven. Salary, hours, vacations, etc., were to be negotiated with the participating institution, on the basis of guidelines suggested in Stallmann's report. The mechanics of administration were thoroughly spelled out; the rationale behind the techniques of the proposal is what must be of concern here.

If a cluster of criteria was applied to the selection of libraries to accept interns, the ones chosen "would be those in which the education of the intern was considered of more importance than the service to be secured from the intern." But this implies finding a library not only superbly staffed to allow for time to carry out this educational function, but blessed with supervisors who are able to teach well. Noting that surveys in the early 1950s confirmed Williamson's earlier observation that comparatively few librarians possess either the time or the skill to teach, Stallmann nevertheless placed her faith in "common knowledge that some excellent library supervisors are employed, some in equally excellent libraries."[47] These professionals, presumably, would be recruited to perform the task of bridging the student's theoretical knowledge with practical insights.

Stallmann's determination to leave as little as possible to chance in matching intern and institution clashed in principle with Reece's observation that field work is most efficacious when most shaped by unpredictability and that "to plan [actual conditions] meticulously and to methodize it thoroughly would be prejudicial."[48] Length of time, also, seemed conveniently gauged to the school's academic calendar; that is, there was an administrative rather than an intrinsically educational rationale for it. If integration of theory with practice was really the goal, there was no empirical method of determining that the training was "just enough to illuminate the principles involved and to cultivate the essential skills, but not so much as to make of learning a profitless repetitive exercise."[49]

Feedback to the school would be minimal under this plan. The participating institution would make a report to the school after the first month of work and at the end of the internship period. In the case of distance precluding personal contact with the teaching faculty, even St. John's "friendly and informal chats" between student and faculty advisor would be impractical or impossible. Of course the master's thesis would ostensibly demonstrate whether the intern realized the integration of theory and practice in his experience, but if unrealized the experience would not be correctable. Of perhaps more importance, Lieberman's objection remained unexplained: supervision of practical work in the hands of persons who have less training than those who expound the theory is difficult to justify as an articulation of pedagogical means and ends.[50] As Reece stated, librarians hold appointment "by reason of fitness for library work, not because of ability to teach";[51] it follows that however excellent the supervision, the primacy of the educational function of the experience would always be in part adventitious.

Ultimately, the fundamental criticism of Williamson goes unsatisfactorily answered in Stallmann's proposal. Under her plan interns were to be selected on a competitive, or prestige, basis. The internship is to be looked upon as an honor; the stipend would then be perceived by the intern as a "fellowship." "It is reasonable . . . for each library to want the best student available" for the internship, and the school would choose accordingly.[52] But Williamson argued that the purpose of integrating theory and practice in any kind of practical work requires, in addition to superior students, the selection of students who have *not* shown proficiency in relating problem solving to theory in normal classroom exercises. If the aim, he said, is to validate expected success in the real world with formal performance in school, "then the type of field work does not greatly matter." Where the best students become interns and perform as expected, no validation of the pedagogical worth of the internship can be assumed. Those students who most need the practical component to fulfill the school's teaching-learning process will be served not at all.[53]

Stallmann's report originated in the University of Texas Graduate School of Library Science, and the school has for a number of years sent interns to participating libraries throughout the United States. Unfortunately, a search of the literature revealed no assessment of the program (theses undertaken and completed under the provisions of this program are listed in *Library Literature* and can be obtained in microform or in hard copy). Despite the unresolved problems in this form of work contact, at least within the theoretical framework of the Williamson and Reece analyses, the study remains singular in its exploration and implementation of a full-fledged project during this period.

With the exception of scattered announcements and news items, little appeared in the literature on the issue of practical work in the curriculum for over a decade. This protracted silence puzzled Samuel Rothstein, who presented a paper on the situation at the International Conference on Librarianship held in 1967 under the auspices of the University of Illinois Graduate School of Library Science. His original intent had been to examine the respective roles "to be allocated to practice work and theory in the present-day library school curriculum"; finding nothing on the subject, he shifted focus to an analysis of reasons the experiential component had become "a forgotten issue" in library education.[54]

Rothstein discovered in the latter half of the sixth decade the same checkered pattern of practical work in the United States and Canada that Williamson had discovered in the early 1920s. Requirements varied considerably among the schools; the length of time ranged from two weeks to fifteen hours per week for ten weeks; some schools offered credit, others did not; some schools called for a supervised practicum for school librarianship, and so forth. The terminological vagaries that annoyed Williamson still prevailed. It appeared, disconcertingly, that the admonitions of Williamson and Reece had been largely ignored.

One pattern, however, emerged clearly: field work "now holds only a minor place in the American library school curriculum." This contrasted markedly with the situation in Great Britain and in other professional curricula on this continent: "Almost without exception, the preparation for other professions calls for a major share of the student's time to be given to practical work." If the disregard of library schools in the United States is patently unrepresentative of policies prevailing generally in professional education, "how do American library schools justify this exceptional position?"

Rothstein surmised that the majority of schools that offer no field work pursue this policy because they are skeptical of its educational value. The argument that programs are too burdensome administratively did not hold for the ten programs in Rothstein's survey which were conducting school-sponsored projects. Nor was lack of control, in Rothstein's judgment, an adequate excuse; some schools had found "enough cooperation and ability on the part of the field staff to ensure students a genuinely educational experience." Other excuses, the author held, such as large enrollments and competition from other subjects in a crowded curriculum, were based upon expedience rather than upon a valid rejection on educational grounds. Rothstein believed that "the majority view derives from history rather than logic."

In Rothstein's opinion, three pejorative connotations of practical work have unduly influenced library educators. Being associated with Dewey and earlier, it has been considered an embarrassing "survival of the apprenticeship era." Secondly, it has usually been managed badly, and repeated criticism has blurred the distinction between what was incompetently done and what could be done well. Finally, and most importantly, it "has come somehow to stand for opposition to theory, and the persistent pursuit of American library education has been to find a curriculum that would emphasize and embody theory."

Rothstein's thesis was that past testimony is not sufficient reason for ignoring the issue of practice in the curriculum. He was persuaded that in overemphasizing theory, library schools had mistaken "trappings for substance. For many librarians and library educators, theory connotes scholarship, practice connotes vocationalism, and the library school programs have ignored the fact that true professionalism calls for both."[55]

Rothstein's attempt to revive the moribund issue of the experiential facet of library education appeared as the latest forceful position in the continuing debate. From Dewey to the present the pendulum has swung back and forth, its oscillations consonant with those described by students of professional education generally. During the 1970s, the love affair of library educators with that congeries of techniques under the rubric of "information science" tended to reduce meaningful discussion of the practical component to negligible proportions. Thus the 1975 Delphi Study about the future of library education contained this brief and dispiriting statement about practice work in the curriculum:

> Several suggestions about the inclusion of practical experience, field study, internship, etc. in the master's program received support, without a very strong indication of optimism about such experiences being included in the curriculum. A majority of participants thought an internship should be available as an elective, and 64 per cent thought it should be required of all students without prior library experience, even if such a requirement led to the lengthening of the master's degree program.[56]

The bland approbation cited above demonstrates that the paucity of creative and imaginative ideas for reconciling theory with dynamic forms of practical experiences still informs the profession as it has for the last half-century.

SUMMARY

Melvil Dewey's insistence on formal training of a practical nature was predicated on the economy effected by systematic study of techniques. A unified perspective, impossible by means of apprenticeship to a specific library, would result in more effective training of potential managerial and administrative personnel. While this principle was not antithetical to one justification for professional training, *viz*, the time-saving aspect of preparation, it removed the school from the broadening influence of university association. When incorporated into the university setting, the early schools Dewey spawned "tended to remain aloof, without intellectual or curricular integration, left alone and little considered, suffered as children of good librarians but hardly considered members of the university family."[57]

The famous Williamson report rudely awoke the existing library schools from their dogmatic slumber. Among Williamson's many recommendations for upgrading the educational content of library training, the one essential pedagogical task was "to give the student . . . as thorough a grounding as possible in the principles underlying practice and methods."[58] Only by imparting the understanding by which to acquire skills, not the skills themselves, could the training be considered worthy of professional status in a university environment.

Following Williamson there appeared a slow but steady professionalization of library education. Despite some confusion in nomenclature, professional education in librarianship became synonymous with graduate education. Due primarily to the influence of the Williamson report, library education currently enjoys stable, if not distinguished, recognition in the academic milieu.

But Williamson did not reject out of hand the place of a practical element in the curriculum, as some have assumed. Rather, he criticized existing schools for not having given thought to the educational principles by which to accept or reject practice in devising a sound curriculum. The fuzzy terminology was in need of clarification; a logical basis for allocation of time to real experiences was not evident; the kinds of assignments given to students to supplement formal class studies were sloppy and haphazard.

Furthermore, assumptions as to the value of "real life" experiences were based more on romance than on logic. Both sides in the theory-practice controversy have failed to give Williamson a careful reading. Far from "throwing out the baby with the bath," Williamson merely stressed that the assignment of priorities to the curriculum be based upon sound pedagogical principles. That a conscious educational philosophy should inform curricular planning was his message to library educators.

It became evident to Reece that a number of library educators had not grasped Williamson's message. Formulations implicit in the Williamson report were made explicit by Reece's taxonomy of work contacts. Of his six "forms" or categories of practical experiences, the first five involved classroom controlled and oriented situations. These formed a circle of instruction which began and terminated with the teacher. Some radiated outward from the classroom in the form of laboratory work, projects, individualized problems or group observation. Some remained enclosed within the classroom, such as case studies or demonstrations. The sixth form, however, consisted of field experiences in which the teaching-learning circle would perforce be broken in space and in time.

On this last category, field work, Reece trained his critical powers. Since the triadic principles of order, control and effective expenditure of time informed Reece's conceptual framework, the nature of field work could not accommodate the logic of the teaching-learning process. With its elements of risk, inappropriate supervision, unpredictability, and the relative absence of a method by which to articulate theory with practice, field work should not be a formal part of the curriculum. Reece did not challenge the value of this experience; he simply demonstrated its inconsistency with pedagogical objectives.[59]

After Reece, attempts to integrate theory and practice in the curriculum took two forms: There were those faculties that, ignoring the admonitions of Williamson and Reece, uncritically continued various structured and unstructured types of "practice work" or "practical work," and there were some schools that heeded the analyses of the two educators but attempted to circumvent the stated objections.

Educators like St. John and Van Deusen generally argued that pedagogical objections were essentially administrative in character — a problem of effort, money and time — rather than intrinsically illogical in the teaching-learning process. Stallmann's ambitious program for an internship relied on overcoming educational dilemmas by close attention to sound management. Though several efforts over the last four decades to construct a viable experience out of school-controlled field work enjoyed degrees of sophistication, the dilemma inherent in resolving extramural experiences and educational principles was never quite resolved.

It is evident that the principal thrust over the last four decades in library education has been to construct a body of theory. The writings of Danton, Metcalf, Lancour, Berelson and others show that the primary concern has been the reduction or elimination of techniques and routines that had no place in a graduate curriculum. While pronouncements like Leigh's on theory and clinical experience, and Metcalf's on the need for an ideal internship, created a surface impression of interest in continuing the theory-practice dialogue, the inescapable fact has been that this problem no longer exercised a majority of library educators. Like trying to square the circle, the efforts to resolve the theory-technique conundrum appeared more taxing than the presumed rewards. In Swank's metaphor, the old chestnut, theory and practice, had been "roasted and re-roasted a thousand times, but never soundly cracked,"[60] and the schools had directed their energies toward more immediately solvable issues.

The proponents of practical experiences in formal studies did not, certainly, abet their somewhat tarnished cause by citing as educational desiderata for field experiences things like "a refreshing change of pace," "confidence," "extremely interesting," and so forth.[61] That attitudinal gains for the beginning members of a profession are splendid is undeniable; that they demonstrate a correlation of experience with theory would be difficult to prove. At the same time, the criticism of a Van Deusen is not altogether off the mark; the administrative machinery in a curriculum is intimately related to its educational success or failure.

It seems evident that most schools, in Grotzinger's phrase, "see value in field work, but are unwilling to relinquish class time or give academic standing to the concept."[62] However the faculties and deans of library schools have arrived at this judgment, it rests confidently on the educational considerations both Williamson and Reece analyzed. Williamson found that in his day "field practice does not sufficiently clinch and check up theories learned from lectures and reading, *but it does seriously interfere with thorough instruction.*"[63] (Emphasis added.) And of the six forms of work contact Reece analyzed, the one category he found most educationally suspect was field work.

But if library schools have a secure theoretical argument for excluding field work, including internships, the act of exclusion does not resolve the theory-practice issue. Medical schools, for example, have rejected the traditional internship only as the viability of the clinical clerkship has been thoroughly demonstrated. Abandonment of the practicum, internship, or other form of field work, with nothing to take its place in library education, is but an ostrich solution to the practice issue in professional preparation. It may be assumed that education for the professions, like nature, abhors a vacuum.

Williamson and Reece were aware of this problem. The essential pedagogical purpose in Reece's categories of work contacts was "to help students to interpret or to build upon their classroom instruction, and to acquire ease in their surroundings and aptness in the attendant operations."[64] Field work was only one of six forms adjudged unsatisfactory; neither Williamson nor Reece sought to foreclose all possibilities of integrating the theoretical content of classroom instruction with illuminated practice. Indeed, the range of possibilities within the curriculum that may be controlled educationally far exceeds the single approach that is field work.

That decades of debate have failed to resolve the theory-practice issue simply places the profession in the healthy position of being forced to return to the early theoreticians of library education. For there have been no more lucid constructions than those of Williamson and Reece. It is to these pioneers that library educators must once again turn for direction and inspiration. Accordingly, an examination of alternatives to field work, within the framework of the teaching-learning process, may yet liberate library educators to seek creative responses to the legitimate demands of an experiential component in the curriculum.

REFERENCES

[1]Lewis B. Mayhew, "Curricular Change in the Professions," *Education for Librarianship: The Design of the Curriculum of Library Schools* (Papers Presented at a Conference on the Design of the Curriculum of Library Schools Conducted by the University of Illinois Graduate School of Library Science, September 6-9, 1970), ed. Herbert Goldhor (Urbana, Illinois: University of Illinois Graduate School of Library Science, 1971), p. 57.

[2]Ibid., p. 53.

[3]Samuel Rothstein, "A Forgotten Issue: Practice Work in American Library Education," *Library Education: An International Survey* (Papers Presented at the International Conference on Librarianship Conducted by the University of Illinois Graduate School of Library Science, June 12-16, 1967), ed. Larry Earl Bone (Urbana, Illinois: University of Illinois Graduate School of Library Science, 1968), pp. 215-16.

[4]William F. Poole, "Supplements to Poole's Index," *Library Journal*, 8 (September-October 1883), 195.

[5]Columbia University School of Library Economy, *Circular of Information, 1886-87*. The program "confines itself strictly to its peculiar work, and makes no attempt to give general culture or make up deficiencies of earlier education. . . . This school is rather a short and purely technical course."

[6]Louis R. Wilson, "Historical Development of Education for Librarianship in the United States," *Education for Librarianship* (Papers Presented at the Library Conference, University of Chicago, August 16-21, 1948), ed. Bernard Berelson (Chicago: American Library Association, 1949), p. 45.

[7]Charles C. Williamson, *Training for Library Service: A Report Prepared for the Carnegie Corporation of New York* (Boston: The Merrymount Press, 1923).

[8]Abraham Flexner, *Medical Education in the United States and Canada* (Boston: The Merrymount Press, 1910).

[9]Williamson, op. cit., pp. 136, 142.

[10]Charles D. Churchwell, "Education for Librarianship in the United States: Some Factors Which Influenced Its Development Between 1919 and 1939," (Unpublished doctoral dissertation, University of Illinois, 1966).

[11]C. Edward Carroll, *The Professionalization of Education for Librarianship with Special Reference to the Years 1940-1960* (Metuchen, New Jersey: The Scarecrow Press, 1970).

[12]Sarah K. Vann, *Training for Librarianship Before 1923* (Chicago: American Library Association, 1961).

[13]Wilson, op. cit., p. 53.

[14]Carroll, op. cit., p. 184.

[15]Lloyd E. Blauch (ed.), *Education for the Professions* (Washington: GPO, 1959), p. 9. *See also* Bernard Berelson (ed.), *Graduate Education in the United States* (New York: McGraw-Hill, 1960), p. 223.

[16]Carroll, loc. cit.

[17]Ibid., p. 220.

[18]Neal Harlow, "Designs on the Curriculum," *Education for Librarianship: The Design of the Curriculum of Library Schools* (Papers Presented at a Conference on the Design of the Curriculum of Library Schools Conducted by the University of Illinois Graduate School of Library Science, September 6-9, 1970), ed. Herbert Goldhor (Urbana, Illinois: University of Illinois Graduate School of Library Science, 1971), p. 7.

[19]Leon Carnovsky, "Education for Librarianship," *Libraries and Librarians of the Pacific Northwest*, ed. Morton Kroll, (Pacific Northwest Library Association Library Development Reports, Vol. 4) (Seattle: University of Washington Press, 1960), pp. 180-81.

[20]Raynard C. Swank, "Sixth-Year Curricula and the Education of Library School Faculties," *Journal of Education for Librarianship*, 8 (Summer 1967), 15.

[21]Williamson, op. cit., pp. 53-55.

[22]Ibid., p. 56.

[23]Ibid., p. 57.

[24]Ibid., pp. 57-58, 61.

[25]Ibid., pp. 53-55, 58, 62, 65.

[26]Ernest J. Reece, *The Curriculum in Library Schools* (New York: Columbia University Press, 1936), p. 122. By relating library education to professional education generally, Reece provided a useful comparative framework. Accordingly, his citations serve as one of the better sources for writings on education in the several professions that is available for the early decades of this century.

[27]Ibid., pp. 123-24.

[28]Ibid., pp. 121, 124-30.

[29]Rothstein, op. cit., p. 217.

[30]Francis R. St. John, *Internship in the Library Profession* (Chicago: American Library Association, 1938), pp. 8, 25-52.

[31]Ibid., pp. 27-29.

[32]Rothstein (op. cit.) observed the interesting bibliographic pattern as it rose and fell throughout the period from 1923 to 1967 and pre-Williamson. His references provide a useful representation of opinion during these years.

[33]J. Periam Danton, *Education for Librarianship: Criticism, Dilemmas and Proposals* (New York: Columbia University School of Library Service, 1946), p. 8.

[34]Herbert Goldhor, "Some Thoughts on the Curriculum of Library Schools," *School and Society*, LXVII (June 12, 1948), 436.

[35]Danton, op. cit., pp. 10, 20-21, 31.

[36]Keyes D. Metcalf, et al., *The Program of Instruction in Library Schools*, (Illinois Contributions to Librarianship No. 2) (Urbana, Illinois: University of Illinois Press, 1943), p. 77.

[37]Harold Lancour, "Discussion," *Education for Librarianship* (Papers Presented at the Library Conference, University of Chicago, August 16-21, 1948), ed. Bernard Berelson (Chicago: American Library Association, 1949), p. 63.

[38]Joseph L. Wheeler, *Progress and Problems in Education for Librarianship* (New York: Carnegie Corporation of New York, 1946), pp. 53-55.

[39]Metcalf, et al., op. cit., pp. 93-94.

[40]Ibid., pp. 50-51.

[41]Neil C. Van Deusen, "Field Work in Accredited Library Schools," *College and Research Libraries*, VII (July, 1946), 250-55.

[42]Robert D. Leigh, "The Education of Librarians," in Alice I. Bryan (ed.), *The Public Librarian* (New York: Columbia University Press, 1952), p. 353.

[43]Lancour, loc. cit.

[44]Ralph W. Tyler, "Educational Problems in Other Professions," *Education for Librarianship* (Papers Presented at the Library Conference, University of Chicago, August 16-21, 1948) ed. Bernard Berelson (Chicago: American Library Association, 1949), p. 28.

[45]Robert D. Leigh (ed.), *Major Problems in the Education of Librarians* (New York: Columbia University Press, 1954), p. 3.

[46]Esther L. Stallmann, *Library Internships: History, Purpose and a Proposal*, (University of Illinois Graduate School of Library Science Occasional Papers, No. 37) (Urbana, Illinois: University of Illinois Graduate School of Library Science, January, 1954), p. 3, citing C. A. Newell and R. F. Will, "What Is An Internship?" *School and Society*, 74 (December 8, 1951), 359.

[47]Ibid., pp. 8, 11, 13-21.

[48]Reece, op. cit., p. 126.

[49]McGrath, op. cit., p. 290.

[50]Myron Lieberman, *The Future of Public Education* (Chicago: University of Chicago Press, 1960), p. 117.

[51]Reece, op. cit., p. 128.

[52]Stallman, op. cit., p. 12.

[53]Williamson, op. cit., p. 58. The idea of the internship as an elitist endeavor is common in library education. *See*, for example, David J. Netz and Don E. Wood, "The Human Element: A Retrospective Evaluation of the OSUL Internship Program," *American Libraries*, 1 (March 1970), 253-54.

[54]Rothstein, op. cit., p. 197.

[55]Ibid., pp. 214-19.

[56]Kenneth E. Vance, et al., "Future of Library Education: 1975 Delphi Study," *Journal of Education for Librarianship*, 18 (Summer 1977), 7-8.

[57]Sydney B. Mitchell, "The Pioneer Library School in Middle Age," *Library Quarterly*, 20 (October 1950), 273.

[58]Williamson, op. cit., p. 64.

[59]Reece, op. cit., pp. 123-30.

[60]Swank, loc. cit.

[61]Rothstein, op. cit., p. 219.

[62]Laura Grotzinger, "The Status of 'Practicum' in Graduate Library Schools," *Journal of Education for Librarianship*, 11 (Spring 1971), 338.

[63]Williamson, op. cit., p. 65.

[64]Reece, op. cit., p. 130.

3

MODES OF INSTRUCTION
IN LIBRARY EDUCATION

INTRODUCTION

It is less difficult to classify and discuss the various modes of instruction than it is to discover the superiority of one over another. Methods vary by discipline as well as by temperament of the instructor. According to Boyd, our differing conceptualizations of teaching exist for three reasons. First, "we lack the knowledge about learning, motivation, social influence and environmental conditioning that could resolve many of the existing educational conflicts." In the second place, "we are unable to agree on the paradigm" which would describe the nature of our goals. Finally, our lack of agreement on a paradigm contributes to disagreement over procedures by which to investigate the merits of such an example or pattern.[1]

Nevertheless, when methods of instruction are examined, both historically and currently, there is enough consensus to form a rough taxonomy. It is generally held, with Dunkin, that "there are only a few basic teaching methods, but the special applications of these methods are legion."[2] Those peculiar to professional education are similar to the ones employed in the liberal arts curriculum but go beyond the latter in order to provide Shera's "irreducible minimum of the vocational"[3] uniquely mandated by the experiential component in the training of professional practitioners.

Instructional strategies may be classified in terms of the possibilities inherent in the teaching-learning process. Where the method suggests that the focus be upon the teacher as the center of the process, the strategies will differ from the method in which the learner becomes the primary focus. A number of techniques employ a combination of these basic situations, and of course there is a great deal of overlapping. The reader should be aware that this deliberately simplified division is presented to facilitate analysis.

Within this framework the major forms of work contacts, excluding field work, that Reece assigned to professional education generally and library education specifically, may be assayed. Of singular consequence for purposes of this study are the possibilities that may inhere in these modes for reconciling the theory-practice dualism. It was argued in the previous chapter that field work as a form cannot satisfy the pedagogical criteria to be included in this model. Consequently, we will analyze and examine the forms that Reece termed *class presentation, problems, observation, projects,* and *laboratory work.* For unlike field work, these forms are course-centered and course-controlled activities. As techniques they presume to carry the instructional burden as well as provide the vehicle for resolving theory and practice, the need peculiar to professional education.

Despite innovations resulting from new technologies or refinements in teaching strategies, Reece's formulations hold up remarkably well. To be sure, the massive educational machine has generated computerized information retrieval systems, audio- or video-tape tutorials, adjunct programming, simulation games, and the like since Reece constructed his taxonomy. But allowing for the new and for variations on traditional strategies, his outline may be profitably used to conceptualize generic instructional activities.

CATEGORIES OF INSTRUCTION

A useful method of analyzing instructional strategies was suggested by the research of Dubin and Taveggia. They organized activities in terms of the extent to which emphasis is placed upon the teacher and the degree to which learning, either individually or within the group, resides primarily in the student. Noting that four decades of research into the activities of the educative process demonstrate "that we really do not know what the linkage is between teaching and learning," Dubin and Taveggia constructed a scale "which at one end emphasizes instructor-centered classroom situations and at the other end emphasizes student-centered learning situations which may or may not be found in a classroom setting." Thus in a broad spectrum of pedagogical situations there are two distinct modes of teaching-learning behavior, "face-to-face instruction" and "independent study."[4] Completing the model to form a trinity requires, of course, the recogniation of combinations of the modes.

Face-to-Face Instruction

In this category there are a variety of explicit strategies: lecture, group-discussion, question-and-answer, etc. But the underlying philosophical assumption that unifies the diversity of methods is one made famous, or notorious, by John Dewey's systematic assault on its validity: the transmission of knowledge.[5] Variations on this model of the process admittedly mitigate the "authoritarian" image of the traditional lecture. Class participation provides some opportunity for activity on the part of the students; there can be strategies for social interaction and "interpersonal encounter" among students and between teacher and students. Derivatives of this method should not obscure the fact, however, that it assumes the primacy and superiority of the instructor, thus placing in his hands the responsibility for selection of subject matter, depth of coverage, balance between content and illustration, and ultimate evaluative authority. The student as passive receptacle largely prevails.

Independent Study

By contrast, methods of independent study shift the focus of authority from the teacher to the student as self-learner: "By definition, independent study delegates to the student primary responsibility for his own learning, and it is found that in practice very few restrictions are employed."[6] The assumption underlying this mode is that basically learning is an individual act, "a set of events which take place entirely within the learner."[7] It involves activity rather than passivity, and when used as a means of growth corresponds to the very nature of freedom.[8]

The degree of freedom in this strategy is crucial to the process. Dubin and Taveggia found two major types of independent study which have received attention in the research literature. They have been institutionalized in most schools as supervised and unsupervised study. The former retains the concept of the teacher as a "resource person," providing learning guidance. The latter places emphasis solely on the learner and assumes that learning can and does take place in the absence of the teacher. Examples of supervised independent study include programmed texts and the "individual-laboratory." These allow for feedback and guidance by an authority person but permit the student, within a time framework, to proceed at his own pace and develop his own learning rhythms. At the far end of the spectrum unsupervised study permits direct interaction between student and the objects of study, be they print or non-print materials.[9] The elements of order, control and supervision become internalized, with the outside evaluative component an end rather than a periodic, on-going phenomenon. Common to both types of independent study is the potential for heuristic learning.

The Dubin-Taveggia construct can be applied to Reece's five forms for analytical purposes. As Reece defined and exemplified the categories,[10] one clearly falls under the face-to-face instruction mode, another represents the supervised and unsupervised independent study method, and the other three forms can be subsumed under a "combination" rubric. Within all categories the possibilities of integrating theory and practice inhere.

APPLICATIONS

Class Presentation

Williamson found that "the lecture method predominates in all library school instruction" although library educators admitted that generally speaking "the best schools and the best teachers make the least use of the lecture." His indictment of this time-honored manner of imparting information, however, was not confined to library education solely: "In all higher and professional instruction the lecture has proved to be the line of least resistance for the poorly prepared, overworked, or unskilled teacher." He allowed for three extenuating circumstances in retaining this mode: large heterogeneous groups precluded experimentation with other instructional strategies; poor textbooks and manuals, or their absence altogether, placed the burden of transmitting knowledge on the teacher; and other academic and professional demands on faculty time left little energy for inspired, creative teaching. For example, class size alone forced instructors to construct examinations that could be swiftly graded. This invariably meant quizzes that emphasized routine processes. Hence, those processes had to be emphasized in class, and a vicious circle rapidly became institutionalized into the curriculum.[11]

Williamson had little else to say on methods of instruction. He was enchanted with the idea of correspondence instruction, and devoted an entire chapter of his report to its advantages.[12] He found reliance upon part-time instructors pedagogically unwise. But his major criticism was leveled at the excessive dependence on the lecture method, which he reiterated in his summary chapter.[13]

Besides his taxonomic contribution to instructional modes, Reece offered few specifics in methodology. One can only surmise that his opinion of the unalloyed use of lecturing was similar to that of his mentor and colleague. Implicit in his examination of forms of instruction is the judicious use of diverse ways of presenting materials in class, of illuminating theory with demonstrations. It would be uncharacteristically inconsistent of Reece if that were not so.

Metcalf, Russell and Osborn found in the lecture method "one of the most efficient plans for presenting general principles," but added that the capability of the teacher was crucial in this respect. Lectures must "be supplemented by practice work in the application and illustration of the principles," but if the instructor is weak, the course will tend to "overemphasize details and problems." In the hands of some instructors, the lecture tends to be "anecdotal in character rather than systematic and thorough." Ironically, in the hands of a charming instructor, who may be knowledgeable or even scholarly, the felicity of the stories told to illustrate a point may cause the student to remember the anecdote and forget "the principle that the lecturer intended it to illustrate."[14]

Class discussion was deemed ineffective at best and profitless at worst, due to the lack of practical experience of the students. Thus student participation became discursive, needlessly argumentative, and generally on a rather low level. A similar complaint was leveled at the question-and-answer technique. The situation proved "unnatural" because students "frequently lack the necessary authoritative information." The main purpose of this technique is "to assist students to clarify and broaden their own ideas through thinking that occurs on the spot." But, save in the hands of a Socrates, it tends to degenerate in practice "into a repetition by the students of material they have memorized in anticipation of the questions that may be asked. . . ." Special guest lectures were given high marks, but for their inspirational rather than pedagogical value.[15]

Wheeler noted, but did not document, a report that a large number of Peabody graduates found the lecture method the most effective instructional technique. But "elsewhere" students rated class discussion best for generating ideas, "provided it is well guided." In another instance, "skillful handling of oral reports . . . proved effective."[16] Here, as in earlier comments, success or failure in the various methods of class presentation was presented as a critical function of the quality of instruction. Accordingly, there was no sound manner of determining, even subjectively, whether the student survived and prospered due to or in spite of the mediating efforts of the teacher.

Danton's critique of the lecture method closely paralleled the advantages and disadvantages Metcalf and his colleagues cited. The method is useful "for the presentation of general principles and historical material" but may be "highly wasteful of the student's time, and hence educationally questionable, if it consists chiefly of material which he could as easily acquire through individual reading, or is largely anecdotal." The question and answer method, where it follows lecture material, may be useful for clarification or codification of ideas; where it is used in conjunction with outside preparation, such as practice work or problems, it may rightly be considered as a combination technique. In any case, Danton held that it "can be satisfactorily utilized only with relatively small groups, say not larger than 25 or 30." At best the class discussion *cum* question-and-answer device was excellent as a mode of instruction, but dangers to its effectiveness could arise if students merely "parrot the words of the teacher or waste time by asking questions out of sheer ignorance."[17]

A good deal of interest has been generated in the case method of class presentation. Shaffer defended the merits of the case as an instructional vehicle in his *Twenty-five Short Cases in Library Personnel Administration.*[18] What began as a modest individual effort by Shaffer to strengthen instruction in a single course area, library administration, has developed and expanded, and its proponents are enthusiastically vocal about its educational effectiveness.

For over half a century case studies have been used as a teaching device at the Harvard Graduate School of Business Administration.[19] In library education, one of the most articulate proselytizers for this technique has been Thomas J. Galvin, formerly a professor at the School of Library Science, Simmons College, Boston, where Shaffer was the school's director. Indeed, Simmons is, perhaps unfairly, institutionally identified with this method of instruction, but many individual instructors in the several schools and departments of library science have adopted the case method in part or wholly in their courses.

The putative success of the method at Harvard Business School, and the prestige that school carries, would suggest its trial as a form of instruction in analogous courses in library education such as business management and administration. But Galvin, to cite the best-known champion of this method, extended the case method to the reference course, and in so doing argued a general theory of the technique. Galvin has written and spoken of this approach in effusive terms: the case method "is aimed . . . squarely at the jugular vein of traditional library education"; the objective "has been nothing less than the radical reformation of the library school curriculum"; the experimental program at Simmons has the "irresistible force of an idea whose time has come."[20]

However quaint it is to find such unabashed enthusiasm for curricular innovation, egregious claims for a process or product often become embarrassingly difficult to defend. The philosophical justification for Galvin's case method resides in the distinction between the problem-centered approach and the content-centered approach to library education. Although collections of case studies are used in the case method, it is incorrect to equate the studies with the method. Nor can the method be deduced solely from examination of the cases themselves; they are merely the vehicle for effecting a problem-centered instructional technique.

That is to say, the process of learning rather than the body of materials to be learned is the crucial distinction. A content-centered course emphasizes the transmission of this body of materials, and the materials are determined by the authority of the teacher. Bruner calls this "the method of assertion and proof."[21] The student absorbs the transmitted package and is judged on his ability to regurgitate it properly upon request. Furthermore, the body of material may be highly theoretical or practical; it may be important or trivial; it may be presented exceptionally well or poorly. All this does not matter; Galvin argues that the pedagogical distinction is one of teacher-centered activity and student passivity.

By contrast, the problem-centered approach focuses upon a problem or group of problems that must be resolved. A body of material is necessarily involved, but the student is not required to reproduce this material in a form he thinks will satisfy the teacher. Rather, the student is judged "solely in terms of his demonstrated capacity to produce viable and defensible solutions to a group of very specific problems."

Different kinds of case studies are subsumed under the case method. The "analytical" or "descriptive" case study seeks to develop generalizations from "typical" situations. The "illustrative" or "exemplary" case study proceeds from some general principle to tangible illustrations or examples. A third, which Galvin labels "the instructional case study" emerged from the development of case method teaching. This latter he finds most suitable for library education.

Like the analytical case study, the instructional model presents a specific instance. Unlike the other vehicles, however, the instructional situation "is constructed primarily for the purpose of posing a problem effectively rather than for the purpose of either providing a basis for generalization or illustrating a principle." Accordingly, the instructional case study "must present a problem in such a way that at least two opposing viable solutions are possible." To find one correct answer is simply not suitable to the model.

This antinomian resolution to problems may be frustrating, especially to beginning students whose thirst for "Answers" is unslakeable. But it has the great advantage of mirroring more faithfully the reality of the pluralistic world. Galvin is not averse to admitting imperfections in the case method. As a form of class presentation it must inevitably be "but an imperfect simulation of reality," although library educators are always too apologetic about this obvious drawback. He cites the "inherent artificiality of the classroom environment" and the danger that the instructor's opinions in the discussion may *ex officio* carry more weight than deserved. "It will be recognized as well that it is one thing for students to make decisions in a protected academic setting, and quite another to have to live with the consequences of these decisions in the world of professional practice." Galvin is persuaded, however, that the advantages far outweigh the disadvantages.

Galvin suggests that the case approach "may have a contribution to make to the formulation of an adequate theoretical structure for librarianship." The case method "can accommodate any valid body of theory or principles that may emerge as a consequence of research into the organization and dissemination of knowledge and information." Since theory needs to be modified and adapted "to fit the requirements of a discipline that is practiced in a real world of multiple variables," the case method affords a highly effective means for testing "the applicability and validity of a theoretical structure."[22] As an instructional method it satisfies the criteria of control and supervision; as an instrument for reconciling theory and practice, some variation on the analytical or exemplary form of the method would appear to serve more usefully than the instructional model that Galvin prefers.

For Ramey the basic shortcoming of the case method is that it is fixed in a two-dimensional condition. The written case exists within the framework of the participants and the facts of the study. Lacking are the dynamics of the developing situation as it evolves through time, that is, the interaction process.

By moving from the static "case" to the dynamic "role playing" technique, some difficulties in methodology can be overcome. But role playing has a disadvantage in that participants are unable to step back out of the role and react to what is happening while it is happening. Ramey resolves this problem by videotaping the role playing case study. The tape then serves as the focus for class discussion.

"Theory sessions" and "problem sessions" ensue after the videotape playback. Ramey claims that this method serves to eliminate the problem of the teacher as "autocratic answer-giver" and the student as passive absorber. While admitting the technique is likely to tax the patience of the teacher, he can serve as catalyst and resource person. The built-in difficulties of the transmission of knowledge in the face-to-face instructional situation are subverted, while the advantages of control and feedback in class presentation are preserved. The problem sessions are analytical, illuminating one or several theoretical concepts. Theory, in turn, bends back upon specific problems which may refine or amplify principles.[23]

Ramey is here commenting on a single course, library administration, but the method could serve all areas of library education where complex problems admit of multiple resolutions illustrative of general principles. Indeed, proponents of role-playing and simulation in library education include Lawson[24] (public library service and administration) and Shuman[25] (reference, intellectual freedom and censorship, job interviewing, and management), who favor this mode of instruction. Both the case study and the simulation method are viable alternatives to the traditional pattern of descriptive instruction, in which a body of information is elevated to the status of a body of knowledge largely by virtue of an authority transmitting this corpus to passive receptables.

Dunkin suggested yet another way to subvert the tendency to transmit information that is articulated by the method of face-to-face instruction. Especially useful for very large classes, he would have the students teach one another. An appealing suggestion, and one which has received critical attention in the literature of pedagogy for children and young adults, Dunkin visualized a class in advanced cataloging employing this technique. To simulate reality, the class "might be divided into small cataloging 'departments' with each member of each group serving as 'head cataloger' for some time, guiding and revising the work of the others in his 'department.'"[26] This strategy has been employed in forms of laboratory work, and the element of the student-as-teacher does have some unexplored novel possibilities. Dunkin does not suggest the defined role of the teacher, but presumably it would be that of guidance and informal direction rather than authoritative transmission.

Sabor agreed with Metcalf that if the teacher is dynamic, the "lecture" is one of the most effective forms of presentation of general principles. In her analysis, the word "lesson" was employed as the generic expository method, to include class discussion, reading and commentary on textual materials, and question and answer as well as the formal lecture. Believing that this fundamental mode had been unfairly belittled in the past, she appealed for its restoration "to its proper importance and, thereby, the importance of the teacher who really teaches."

According to Sabor, the effectiveness of this medium of instruction could be fulfilled only if two essential conditions obtained: "that it be used for the genuinely theoretical part of the teaching and the subjects in which practical work plays a minor part, and secondly, that the teachers have the qualities required for giving it: sound training, synthesizing ability, expository talent, ease of communication and professional experience"; that is, if both subject matter and teaching skill defined the parameters of the method. Most appropriate to the lesson procedure were the "core subjects" which provided the introduction to librarianship. Sabor argued cogently for this technique given the above circumstances; the teacher must transmit superior knowledge and so order it that students may receive the "word" in logical context: "Only thus will the proper priorities be established between technique and theory. . . ."[27]

Authorities agree that the varieties of class presentation represent the primary vehicle of instruction *ex cathedra*. Refinements of this didactic structure, including forms of the case method, represent a shift in control and participation from teacher to student. But the logical order is that of the teaching cycle, which begins in presentation and ends with provision for the association of the student in the development of the process. Whether the development is problem-centered or content-centered, passive or in part active, the form is held to be not only logical but pedagogically sound.

Problems

Reece defined problems as "consisting essentially of unsupervised course work," such as the *projet* in architecture education.[28] Following Dubin and Taveggia, however, one can render Reece's form more precise by analyzing the degree of supervision involved in forms of independent study. Though academic offerings of this kind are usually given a course number for administrative purposes, the standard elements of class presentation are usually absent. Generally, too, this method comes toward the end or at the end of a program of study, when the student has mastered the theoretical insights, skills, and confidence to assume a greater share of responsibility in the learning process.

Supervised Independent Study

When used as an adjunct to class presentation, assigned problems have been a staple of all courses in library education that have "practical" application: reference and bibliography, selection, classification and cataloging. A form of "homework," the investigation of materials, classifying books, and the like are performed unassisted or in groups. In these assignments the teacher generally knows the "answer" or what the end of the process should yield. In this situation the element of independence is vitiated by its having been staged. The orchestration of problems by the teacher is a legitimate pedagogical strategy, but it does not properly fall under the heading "independent study," even though it may have been independently achieved.

There is a surprising paucity of commentary in library literature on independent study. This is especially odd in view of the criticism of library education early and late as stifling, oriented to the trivial, rule and rote dominated. Yet virtually all schools make provision for independent study in their catalog offerings. It appears that perhaps its very "taken-for-granted" characteristic has inhibited a critical examination of its educational potential. Or, like the tutorial system that American educators admire from afar when they picture the Oxford don and his young charge, the consequences of independent study are luxuries to be infrequently indulged.

Yet if some of the pedagogical shortcomings of class presentation are made inevitable by the very structure of that mode, the forms of independent study might serve to liberate library education from its excessive reliance on the group experience. To be sure, the standard disclaimer is the argument of faculty time and size of the student body. Similar to Van Deusen's rejoinder on field work, however, this argument may be viewed as an administrative problem that has no intrinsic relation to educational merit or lack thereof.

The supervised aspect of independent study is tutorial and directed; the instructor provides structured guidance. Unlike unsupervised independent study, this method has a built-in necessity for teacher-directed participation in the learning process. Depending on the degree of structure in the guidance, the teacher communicates a model of expected performance. The emphasis is on the learner, but the teacher is active "as a motivator, a transmitter of values, and a guide to outlines, indexes, reference lists and other materials or devices designed for imparting knowledge to the student."[29]

Motivational or attitudinal enhancement aside, the elements of control and supervision are present in the method, while the advantages in the teacher's construction of a framework in which the student can relate the theoretical and practical are legion. The assumption, presented as a given, is that a problem or cluster of problems worthy of graduate level pursuit in professional education is amenable to a revelation of both theory and technique.

Unsupervised Independent Study

Lacking in this basic teaching-learning strategy is the critical element of periodic control: "The role of the instructor is limited to constructing bibliographies and materials relevant to the particular subject matter."

Then the students "must fare for themselves."[30] Normally, an oral or written examination or research paper is required at the end of the problem. But the uneasiness of Reece and others about uncontrolled and unsupervised practical experiences is appropriate here. There is no vehicle by which the teacher can monitor and guide theoretical insights that may have gone unrecognized. A popular kind of assignment in this vein is the preparation of a lengthy bibliography on a topic. Whether the bibliography is adequate or inadequate, there is no opportunity, for example, for the instructor to know if the student has gained any insight into the nature of bibliography and of the bibliographic universe.

If the injection of greater amounts of independent study into a curriculum is patently impossible from an administrative, cost-accounting viewpoint, there are modes in which elements of this technique can be absorbed. Indeed, a combination of the best pedagogical values of class presentation and independent study would be superior to the exclusive employment of one or the other.

Observation

Field work, which necessarily incorporates observation, was criticized by Williamson for not allowing close and critical examination of the total unit, so that understanding of interrelated activities was missed. But in conjunction with classroom training, Reece acknowledged observation as a useful component in the instructional process. Without implying that he had exhausted the possibilities, Reece cited two examples of this method, visits to illustrate a subject matter being studied and trips to observe an entire organizational unit. The former was exemplified by a visit to a classed catalog by a group studying cataloging; the latter by a visit to a system, or a number of libraries, perhaps undertaken by the entire library school.[31]

Metcalf et al. averred that observation is a salutary form of instruction, but pointed out that its value "is likely to be in proportion to the degree of supervision that is exercised by capable members of the teaching staff."[32] Just as the judicious selection of examples brought into the classroom depends upon the organizing talent of the teacher, so the teacher in the observable experience must make, in Buberian terms, a logical "selection . . . of the effective world."[33]

Metcalf and his colleagues cited two opposing views of the time when observation might be most effective. One school of thought insisted that, "to be most profitable, the experience must be given shortly after the student has mastered the most important theoretical concepts related to library science. Students should be carefully prepared for the observation, so that they will know what they are to look for and will recognize and identify what they see."

Another view held that observational experiences are the very first step in the formal preparation: "It is claimed that students by such means may be led to formulate the questions and problems that need answering in the professional curriculum, and that the later studies of the more theoretical sort may be vitalized for the student by this early contact with the realities of the practical situation." That is, an undifferentiated impression of activities, if observed with acuity, would provide a gestalt by which to validate or invalidate, in later formal training, the theoretical assumptions. As a prior consumer of library service the student, of course, has "observed," but observation has been uncritical and unsystematic. Concerning this latter approach, the authors suggested that the idea "might be worthy of exploration in the field of library school instruction."[34]

Danton recognized the experiential value of field trips, or supervised observation. Their purpose, he noted, "is to enable the student to secure a modicum of acquaintance with each of the major kinds of libraries and its services and, while this purpose can be to some extent met through lecture and reading, there is nothing quite so helpful to understanding as seeing with one's own eyes." To be limited in time and to include "at least one good representative library of each major type within the school's orbit," the trips should be preceded by reading and lecture, in order that the principles be understood for more intelligible observation. Class discussion and reports should follow as reinforcement and analysis.[35]

Observation, according to Sabor, provided "for the simplest form of contact with the reality of the field of work selected by the student." Inspection of actual libraries and books, for Sabor, formed "an essential part of the process which will give the student a direct line with — an acclimatization to — his sphere of study and work."

The process of observation itself may be divided into three categories: free from control, guided, or a combination of the two. The educational goal is to instruct the student in the techniques of observation so that he may move from guidance toward freedom as his interest and capacity permit. Because observation "is supposed to direct the subject's attention to a particular object or process, it becomes necessary to fix the end sought with precision and to teach the student how to observe." In Sabor's view, the sector of observable objects and processes was clearly defined and delimited. Therefore, the logical form of this mode contained the pedagogical means and ends for successful teaching and learning. Sabor, with Danton, held this method of instruction valuable in the range of "participative didactic structures."[36]

Projects

If observation is a direct experience of a particular situation or problem, it is also a passive experience. When one turns to the form Reece labeled projects, there is the opportunity to introduce oneself into the process and experience it from within. The shift is from passivity to activity, from observation to inquiry.

Projects share some of the instructional strategies of the other forms in Reece's taxonomy. They include, but go beyond, observation. They may take "the form of problems and sometimes [are] performed under laboratory conditions." They may be "managed most advantageously if built into a course," that is, if they are related to the structure of class presentation. And they are not to be confused with field work, though they partake of the practical element.[37] Projects in library education may bear the same relationship to field work as the clinical clerkship in medical education bears to the internship.

Where a series of projects are related within a unified problem area, the seminar form of instruction is often used. Although the seminar has been defined as "the pinnacle of university training," the "highest form of the university's didactic structure,"[38] there are a variety of less magisterial instructional strategies that can be employed in its conduct. The projects, for example, may be related broadly or generically, but the divergencies of individual effort on the part of the students may be such that, in effect, the seminar becomes a sequence of discrete units of independent study. At the other end of the scale, there may be a totality of effort involved, replete with cooperative researching and writing. Classes may meet for every assigned session, or infrequently. Guidance by the teacher may be active or passive, disinterested or involved, obtrusive or non-directive.

There is, however, a certain consensus on goals and the mechanics of administration: "Students are expected to make important contributions to the development of a somewhat specialized subject."[39] The seminar is effective "only for very small groups" and is "a device of value principally for the more advanced rather than the elementary subject."[40] It is only appropriate to the student who has "already mastered the basic groundwork of subject matter related to the course," and it often contributes to research pursued by the teacher to add to the body of knowledge of the discipline.[41]

Ideally, the goals and administrative structure should obtain. In reality this is not always the case. Metcalf et al. found that "surprisingly few of even the advanced students are able to make really worth-while contributions in library school seminar courses." If one of the instructional strategies is to have students read their papers in class, "the presentation of the report . . . is frequently not as valuable to the other students . . . as the same amount of time spent in other types of instructional activities."[42] No overwhelming evidence exists to suggest that the situations Metcalf commented on have dramatically changed for the better.

If formal presentation of papers in a seminar class is too stilted a device, discussion is not. Patterson observed that "an essential characteristic of the seminar is that its members do original research and that reporting and sharing of discoveries is done in the presence of all the members and the seminar leader."[43] But the method of discussion cannot be left to chance. Line noted that discussion takes place "only when it concerns itself with what is genuinely and importantly doubtable and moves forward to broader and deeper understandings. . . . It is a process of making the culture over in transmissions and in transformation. . . . Knowledge is my knowledge, but always partial; and needs to be challenged by yours, and can grow in wisdom and understanding by discussion among us."[44]

The small class size and the freedom the seminar method provides for both teacher and learner should make it a useful vehicle—used alone or in combination with other instructional modes—for integrating theory and practice in the curriculum. It can be, and has been, used "in all subject areas and at all levels," but usually only after the basic skills or "core" have been completed by the student. Indeed, Patterson found that the seminar method is widely used in graduate library education, "particularly in those courses which emphasize theory, issues and trends in librarianship."

"Case-taught courses" constitute one category where projects are incorporated into a seminar format and employ the problem-centered approach. Here the value of discussion is evident; Line's acknowledged virtue of unpredetermined or even undeterminable ends coincides with Galvin's emphases on open-ended dialogue and pluralistic resolutions, rather than solutions, of problems. In this mode, each case study comprises a "project." The series of projects may be related to a problem or problem areas, or may be discrete in each instance. In this form, however, the necessity of admitting students who have completed certain basic skill- or theory-oriented courses is not cogently felt, for the inquiry process involved can lead from specific facts to theoretical considerations without prior traditional formulations.[45]

Concerning the foregoing, the teaching-learning process begins with the orientation in the class and moves out to the objects of study. The circle is completed with analysis of the learning experiences, the teacher's synthesizing and moderating those experiences in an attempt to effect resolutions either through discussion or student presentation. These "transmissions and transformations" close the circle but do not necessarily, or even desirably, result in solutions or "answers."

If the objects of study are textual, this vehicle grants a potential for integrating theory and actuality. But this integration is second-hand, mediated through materials that are themselves commentaries upon basic experience. If projects involve contact with primary experiences, the opportunities for immediacy in integrating theory and actuality are made more tangible and vivid.

Laboratory Work

Often when library educators comment upon laboratory work as an effective way to achieve educational objectives, they mean nothing more than the traditional handling and inspection of pieces in a collection. The subjects most frequently mentioned in the literature, that appear most suitable to this mode, are cataloging and classification, reference and bibliography. Thus in a laboratory experience devoted to cataloging and classification, "a student would be given books which present different problems of entry, description and subject determination. The problems to be worked on would normally have been considered and discussed in a previous lecture, and in the laboratory period, under the guidance of the instructor, the student would perform the complete processes of cataloging and classification of the books assigned to him." Similarly, for reference and bibliography, following a lecture on the salient characteristics of a tool—purpose, scope, authority, etc.—the student "would be given a series of reference and bibliographical questions and would be expected to find the answers to them."[46] Ingenious variations on this pattern have been devised over the years, but the basic strategy remains the same.

Where the "laboratory" is simply "out there," those materials residing in a library for the purpose of meeting the informational and educational needs of its clientele, the assignments more properly may be subsumed under the "homework" aspect of class persentation. This is especially true of the handling and inspection of large numbers of reference sources and bibliographical tools. In the traditional pattern, the experiences gained by touching, looking at, or perusing the primary sources are supposed to enhance learning. The method is a half-way house between observation and actual practice work. With cataloging and classification, the teaching-learning process may be refined to include a manipulative element; by organizing a "practice collection" of materials, the student allegedly would be learning by doing.

In scientific education the laboratory method is so universally accepted that little research has been done to determine if it is, in fact, a more effective way of achieving educational objectives than other instructional modes. Comparative studies between learning by lecture-demonstration, by laboratory-manual, by problem-solving, and by individual versus group laboratory are inconclusive. The research does suggest, however, that the more understanding of concepts and general problem-solving procedures the instructor emphasizes in the laboratory situation, the more completely principles and scientific attitudes were internalized.[47]

In theory, the method of laboratory instruction should contribute positively to learning. Danton suggested that the reason for including a laboratory experience in library education is identical to that for subjects like chemistry and physics: the learning of a skill or process cannot be sufficiently accomplished by lecturing about it.[48] The definition and rationale provided by Metcalf, et al. is authoritative and comprehensive enough to cite:

> The situation in which students carry on their learning experience through the manipulation of materials under the direct observation and supervision of the instructor is known as the laboratory method. The great advantage in this method is that the teaching may be concrete and may deal with the actual

objects, substances, or processes about which the student is to learn, rather than with mere abstract discussion of them. The manipulative processes engaged in may have direct transfer value to some practical situation and the student may thus acquire useful skills as well as theoretical knowledge. The waste of learning through error that may result in such a situation may be kept at a minimum by careful supervision.[49]

This definition would preclude experiences of handling and inspecting material in an unspecified location. Furthermore, it would suggest that certain courses such as cataloging and classification, in which small illustrative materials in a practice collection can be gathered, are more amenable to laboratory work than courses such as advanced materials in the social sciences. The deliberate minimization of error by supervision reinforces Reece's statement that "Laboratory work, although lacking the discovery element, has come to wide acceptance by teachers of cataloging as a means for supplementing class presentation."[50]

Reece and Metcalf touch upon a difficult problem here. If theoretical knowledge (as well as skills) is to be gained in the laboratory experience, McGrath's question of *How much experience?* is a pertinent one. To find the ideal time span that will permit illumination of principles and realize a certain proficiency in processes involves sound judgment on the part of both teacher and student. If, as Metcalf pointed out, the laboratory mode involves a "heavy drain on the instructor's time," the consumption of time must be abridged in the student's trial-and-error sequence arbitrarily, that is, extrinsic to pedagogical objectives. The rule of thumb, three hours of laboratory for one hour of "lecture" in terms of units of credit,[51] is an inherently administrative consideration. It may be adequate for one person; for another it may be crucial in denying his "use of the heuristic hunch" as a means of relating principle and process.[52] Overt restrictions on discovery in the teaching-learning process may be necessary but cannot be necessarily adjudged a value.

According to Metcalf, the chief drawback to laboratory work, at least in the area of cataloging, is that the experience "does not sufficiently simulate actual conditions in a catalog department."[53] Dunkin concurred with this observation. Noting that laboratory practice is generally conducted as a combination method of face-to-face instruction and supervised independent study, Dunkin questioned the practical value of the experience: "The catch in the argument is that the student is still working under very artificial conditions. The cataloging he learns bears the mark of the laboratory teacher, not necessarily the mark of any 'real live' library in the world."[54]

Again one is faced with a dilemma. Laboratory work insidiously slides into practical work as simulation more closely approximates a real situation: "The purpose of . . . [practical work] parallels closely . . . the purposes of the laboratory: the student learns by doing, he observes at first hand how library operations are carried on, for what purposes and with what results, and he relates practical situations, needs, and problems to what he has learned from lecture and reading and to the more theoretical approach of the classroom."[55]   But as simulation becomes more "real," the perennial problems of uncertainty, lack of control and supervision, difficulty of articulation with theory, and parochial emphases—i.e., the absence of the holistic approach—gain greater probability.

Daily suggests, in an extraordinarily negative and petulant diatribe, that the confusion of laboratory work with on-the-job training and with homework persists.[56] In Part I of his polemic on library education, published in May, 1972, he compared, unfavorably, the clinical training in medical education with similar attempts in library education. "Some teachers," he noted, "have observed that giving homework which must be done in the library has some of the effect of clinical practice." But the loss of control by the school, plus the "undisguised hatred" of the university librarian whom the students descend upon, results in an unhappy pedagogical experience. In the case of adequate practice collections in library school libraries used as laboratories, the assumption of set tasks that could be performed nowhere else caused a security problem. To the extent that the teacher used the same examples from the collection, the underground grapevine built up the "answers," much like the time-honored fraternity collection of old examinations which an indolent professor might dust off and use again.

Where the library-as-laboratory relies upon discards from the University Library to build up its practice collection, teachers must make a haphazard effort to create theory-illuminated exercises. Control is lost, in that suitability at a given moment is to an extent adventitious. Experimental searches are limited, as is the heuristic element. If the students, alternatively, are sent to the university library, the experience no longer becomes a laboratory one, and the seemingly ubiquitous conflict between the professional staff and library students is exacerbated.

Thus Sabor considered it essential   "to equip the library schools with laboratories, whatever the level to which it is sought to train the students. The latter will thus have the use of selected material, ordered rationally to match the gradual increase in the magnitude of the difficulties to be overcome, or the complexity of the cases to be settled."[57] But she noted, of course, that the cost of maintaining such a facility and the suitability of space are crucial factors in realizing the educational efficacy of this method of instruction.

SUMMARY

When applying the Dubin-Taveggia model to the Reeceian taxonomy, we find that the several varieties of *class presentation*, with the possible exception of the case study, emphasize the authority of the teacher in the educative process. The lecture method holds a central place in the didactic structure of class presentation, but there are so many variations of the "lecture" that what constitutes the method is not as obvious as it would appear. Wallen and Travers concluded that "about the most definitive statement one can make about the lecture method is that during most of the time the instructor is 'talking to' the students."[58] A number of library educators have considered the lecture an effective instrument for conveying theory and principles but agree that the abundant skills of the teacher are crucial to the success or failure of the strategy. Almost alone, however, Williamson found little redeeming merit in this technique.

Class discussion begets ambivalent feelings among educators; one survey indicated that some found it wasteful if students were unprepared or the interaction was trivial. Again the consensus was that relatively few teachers are talented enough to perform within this structure with great effectiveness. Moreover, the range of variation among instructors in combining lecture with the several strategies of discussion was so great that "one man's lecture may be another man's discussion."[59]

The basic process of the case method has been that of identifying the principles which underlie particulars. Galvin recognized several assumptions about the profession of librarianship commonly held by those favoring the case method: the emphasis on the practical, or applied, nature of librarianship; its status as an "emerging discipline" lacking a substantial body of knowledge; its dynamic aspect, owing to changing social needs and the impact of new technologies; its interdisciplinary and eclectic character; and the like.[60] Although the logical order in the case study method is controlled by the structure the teacher assigns to the learning process, the emphasis on problem solving rather than on a body of material to be transmitted shifts the focus from passive absorption to active inquiry. While Ramey, among others, would refine the process by introducing role playing and videotaped playback sessions, the general theory of methodology holds.

Modes of instruction *ex cathedra* are modified if not abandoned within the broad category of independent study. This classification yields to degrees of freedom on a scale with numerous gradations. Supervised independent study can be found in the traditional homework assignments. Unsupervised independent study places great freedom but equally great responsibility on the student. This form of experience in Reece's schema is called *problems*, and the category embraces all cognitive activities, supervised or unsupervised, in which the student is the primary agent of his own learning experiences.

In the sense that problems are contrived (that is, teacher-initiated with predictable outcomes), they are not properly a function of independent study. Danton was correct when he noted that the student tends to lose interest when the problems "have little or no relationship to real-life situations."[61] The legitimacy of independent study depends upon the extent to which the student initiates the problem and develops patterns of inquiry. The teacher may convey a sense of expected goals and provide a model. Indeed, a provided structure may cohere with more viscosity than obtains in variant forms of class presentation. But the focus of the process is the learner.

For this mode the level of sophistication of the student is a critical factor in the degree of supervision deemed necessary or warranted. But unsupervised study pursued independently lacks the element of periodic control. Unless student-initiated, there is little opportunity for the teacher to discover whether theory has illuminated techniques at critical incidents in the heuristic process.

Observation, a time-honored form of supplementing class presentation, is initially useful only to the extent that the student is taught how to observe systematically. Some suggest that students, being prior consumers of library service, have observed the system in operation and are already capable of formulating questions to which theory and principles can be assigned.[62] My opinion is that students, before entering library school, rarely view the library with anything approaching a pattern of systematic scrutiny. It is theoretically possible that an amorphous series of impressions may be sufficient for subsequent critical analysis, but such an absence of direction is of dubious pedagogical value.

Observation may begin with precise and structured guidelines and move toward greater student autonomy in the methods and objects of observation. Lynch and Whitbeck reported success in student observation at the reference desk. An analysis of what students observed showed that a large number gave "a great deal of thought . . . in relating their observations 'on the floor' to their assigned theoretical readings."[63] Since some library activities and processes can be operationally defined, library educators seem to agree that the method is useful in elucidating principles from the observed data.

Projects generally connote work within some experiential context, ideally in an actual rather than simulated environment. Whether related to a common problem area or composed of discrete tasks, the seminar form of class presentation serves as a sound didactic structure. A number of library educators hold that projects in a seminar setting are successful teaching-learning devices only if students are pursuing advanced studies and can draw upon the basic theory and principles they presumably learned in the earlier courses. While little has been written on the seminar method in the literature of education, lofty and abstract statements have been made in its behalf.[64] Projects pursued independently or in groups, appropriately discussed and integrated with theoretical concerns in the seminar meetings, would appear to provide a robust vehicle for the integration of theory and practice. As projects approach an actual condition or case, even though simulation may be necessary, the resolution of theory with reality can be more meaningfully articulated.

Gagne observed that in its most general sense, *laboratory work* is "an instructional mode whose purpose is to present a stimulus situation that brings the student into contact with actual objects and events. Although familiarly associated with education in science, the laboratory in this broad meaning can equally well be a part of instruction in almost any subject. . . . In contract to other instructional modes, the laboratory uses actual objects and events for stimuli, rather than verbal communications about them."[65]

Thus broadly conceived, educators of library and information science have defined laboratory work to include the mere handling and inspection of materials in a practice collection, usually located in a corner of the library school library. Practice in the processes of cataloging and classifying books appears most prominently as illustrations of the method in the literature; reference and bibliographical perusal of tools to a slightly lesser extent. Laboratory work has also been equated with field work or with homework in the sense that the university library is a laboratory in macrocosm, like the real world.

Properly defined, however, the laboratory should be specifically located and precisely delimited in tasks and goals. There appears to be agreement that contacts with the objects and events of this "reality" permit, under controlled conditions of learning, the acquisition of useful skills as well as theoretical knowledge. If the resolution of the theoretical component is not evidently or rapidly achieved, the reality base for learning processes is clearly present. Given the inevitable restrictions of time on student and teacher, the mediating effort of the latter is a crucial variable in the appropriate allocation of practice and principle.

A perennial criticism of laboratory work is that it does not sufficiently mirror actual conditions of practice. But that judgment tends to overlook the cogent arguments of Williamson and Reece against an apotheosis of the false goal of "actual conditions." As one approaches the essentially random reality of conditions in actual work, the opportunities for controlled and systematic teaching are diminished.[66]

Unlike laboratory experiences in science education, the uses of this mode in library training have been relatively unsophisticated. Often the "practice collection" has depended for its existence on materials discarded by the university library, personal collections of the faculty, or gifts and exchanges. But, as Sabor indicated, the installation and upkeep of a truly first-rate laboratory have been deemed too costly.[67]

Interestingly, this argument from cost is the same used to spurn organized field experiences. But field work has been rejected by Reece on the grounds of unsound pedagogy. The latter objection, however, appears not to obtain in the laboratory experience. Under appropriate conditions, the potential for systematic, controlled and supervised learning exists. Student and instructor can gauge the amount of practice necessary to educe a principle in a defined location under school administration, not subject to fortuitous elements in extramural settings. In short, the McGrath criteria — *What kind of experience?, How much?*, and *When?* — and the question *Where?* can be satisfied within the logical framework of educational aims and objectives.

Observation, projects, and *laboratory work* are the three forms of the experiential component best suited to strategies that combine the Dubin-Taveggia categories of face-to-face instruction and independent study. Moreover, the Reeceian forms of work contacts permit numerous structures in employing modes of instruction to integrate theory and practice. However clamorously the relative merits of methodology are argued, it is difficult to refute Peters' statement that any "educational situation involves essentially a contrived and controlled environment."[68] Moreover, the absence of clear evidence that shows one method superior to another should not provide educators with an excuse to suspend experimentation in curricular innovation.[69]

As for field work, Reece's bête noire, evidence of its popularity continues to appear in the literature like weeds in a garden. But any sustained program of field work usually creates a problem of concurrent versus deferred experience. In other modes, such as the laboratory concept, articulation of theory and practice can take place both within a course and within the total curriculum, thus negating the disadvantages of pre-school or post-school work, whether that work be called practicum, internship, field training, etc.[70]

That the task is difficult was voiced by Coughlin over a decade ago. His admixture of frustration and hope suggests cautious optimism for the future:

> Those who hope to find answers to the problem of improving library school teaching will, I am afraid, be disappointed. We can, however, take some comfort in the fact that others have been searning for the answers to the same general problem for at least two decades without noticeable success. Perhaps future discussion will provide at least tentative answers to some of the problems plaguing us.[71]

REFERENCES

[1]Robert D. Boyd, "General Principles of Teaching at the University Level," *Library Education: An International Survey* (Papers Presented at the International Conference on Librarianship Conducted by the University of Illinois Graduate School of Library Science, June 12-16, 1967), ed. Larry Earl Bone (Urbana, Illinois: University of Illinois Graduate School of Library Science, 1968), p. 225.

[2]Paul Dunkin, "Good Teaching Methods in Library School Instruction," *Library Education: An International Survey*, op. cit., p. 273.

[3]Jesse H. Shera, "Theory and Technique in Library Education," *Library Journal*, 85 (May 1, 1960), 1736.

[4]Robert Dubin and Thomas C. Taveggia, *The Teaching-Learning Paradox: A Comparative Analysis of College Teaching Methods* (Eugene, Oregon: Center for the Advanced Study of Educational Administration, University of Oregon, 1968), pp. 3, 27-30.

[5]John Dewey, *Experience and Education* (New York: Collier Books, 1963), p. 17. "The subject-matter of education consists of bodies of information and of skills that have been worked out in the past; therefore, the chief business of the school is to transmit them to the new generation."

[6]Dubin and Taveggia, op. cit., p. 29.

[7]Ibid.

[8]Dewey, op. cit., pp. 61-65.

[9]Dubin and Taveggia, op. cit., pp. 29-30.

[10]Reece, pp. 123-24.

[11]Williamson, pp. 40-41.

[12]Ibid., pp. 114-20.

[13]Ibid., p. 138.

[14]Keyes D. Metcalf, et al., *The Program of Instruction in Library Schools* (Illinois Contributions to Librarianship, No. 2) (Urbana, Illinois: University of Illinois Press, 1943), p. 38.

[15]Ibid., pp. 39-40, 53.

[16]Joseph L. Wheeler, *Progress and Problems in Education for Librarianship* (New York: Carnegie Corporation of New York, 1946), pp. 50-51.

[17]J. Periam Danton, *Education for Librarianship* (Unesco Public Library Manuals, I) (Paris: Unesco, 1949), pp. 27-28.

[18]Kenneth Shaffer, *Twenty-five Short Cases in Library Personnel Administration* (Hamden, Connecticut: Shoe String Press, 1960).

[19]Malcolm P. McNair and Anita C. Hersum (eds.), *The Case Method at the Harvard Business School* (New York: McGraw-Hill, 1954).

[20]Thomas J. Galvin, "A Case Method Approach in Library Education," *Library School Teaching Methods: Courses in the Selection of Adult Materials* (Proceedings of a Conference on Library School Teaching Methods Held at the University of Illinois, September 8-11, 1968), ed. Larry Earl Bone (Urbana, Illinois: University of Illinois Graduate School of Library Science, 1969), pp. 60-61.

[21]Ibid., p. 62, citing Jerome S. Bruner, *The Process of Education* (New York: Vintage Books, 1960), p. 21.

[22]Ibid., pp. 21, 62-63, 68-71.

[23]James W. Ramey, "Simulation in Library Administration," *Journal of Education for Librarianship*, 8 (Fall, 1967), 86, 88-89.

[24]Barry R. Lawson, "An Educational Simulation Model of Public Library Service," *Journal of Education for Librarianship*, 14 (Fall 1973), 96-106.

[25]Bruce A. Shuman, "Role-Playing and Simulation in Library School Courses," *Library Scene*, 5 (September, 1976), 9-11.

[26]Dunkin, op. cit., p. 287.

[27]Josefa E. Sabor, *Methods of Teaching Librarianship*, Unesco Manuals for Libraries, 16 (Paris: Unesco, 1969), pp. 86-89.

[28]Reece, op. cit., p. 124.

[29]Dubin and Taveggia, loc. cit.

[30]Ibid., p. 30.

[31]Reece, op. cit., p. 125.

[32]Metcalf et al., op. cit., p. 51.

[33]Martin Buber, *Between Man and Man* (New York: MacMillan, 1965), p. 89.

[34]Metcalf et al., op. cit., pp. 51-52.

[35]Danton, op. cit., p. 31.

[36]Sabor, op. cit., pp. 53-54.

[37]Reece, op. cit., pp. 124-25.

[38]Sabor, op. cit., pp. 57-58.

[39]Metcalf et al., op. cit., p. 54.

[40]Danton, op. cit., p. 28.

[41]Metcalf et al., loc. cit.

[42]Ibid., pp. 54-55.

[43]Charles D. Patterson, "The Seminar Method in Library Education," *Journal of Education for Librarianship*, 8 (Fall, 1967), 99.

[44]Ibid., pp. 99-100, citing William Line, "A Discussion of Discussion," *Improving College and University Teaching*, 10 (Autumn, 1962), 204-205.

[45]Galvin, loc. cit.

[46]Danton, op. cit., p. 29.

[47]W. J. McKeachie, "Research on Teaching at the College and University Level," *Handbook of Research on Teaching*, ed. N. L. Gage (Chicago: Rand McNally and Co., 1963), pp. 1144-45.

[48]Danton, op. cit., pp. 29-30.

[49]Metcalf et al., op. cit., p. 41.

[50]Reece, loc. cit.

[51]Metcalf et al., op. cit., pp. 41-42; *see also* Danton, op. cit., p. 29.

[52]Jerome S. Bruner, "After John Dewey, What?," *Selected Educational Heresies*, ed. William F. O'Neill (Glenview, Illinois: Scott, Foresman and Co., 1969), p. 353.

[53]Metcalf et al., op. cit., p. 42.

[54]Dunkin, op. cit., p. 282.

[55]Danton, loc. cit.

[56]Jay E. Daily, "Teaching the Rotton Core," *Library Journal*, 97 (May 15, 1972), 1781.

[57]Sabor, op. cit., pp. 95-96.

[58]Norman E. Wallen and Robert M. W. Travers, "Analysis and Investigation of Teaching Methods," *Handbook of Research on Teaching*, op. cit., p. 481.

[59]Ibid.

[60]Thomas J. Galvin, "Problem-Oriented Approaches in the Education of Librarians," *Special Libraries*, 66 (January, 1975), 3-4.

[61]Danton, op. cit., p. 30.

[62]Metcalf et al., op. cit., pp. 51-52.

[63]Mary Jo Lynch and George W. Whitbeck, "Work Experience and Observation in a General Reference Course—More on 'Theory vs. Practice,' " *Journal of Education for Librarianship*, 15 (Spring, 1975), 275.

[64]Patterson, op. cit., p. 100; *see also* Sabor, op. cit., pp. 57-58.

[65]Robert M. Gagne, *The Conditions of Learning* (New York: Holt, Rinehart and Winston, Inc., 1965), p. 291.

[66]Williamson, op. cit., pp. 61-62; Reece, op. cit., pp. 125-27.

[67]Sabor, op. cit., p. 96.

[68]R. S. Peters, *Ethics and Education* (Glenview, Illinois: Scott, Foresman and Co., 1969), p. 116.

[69]Wallen and Travers, op. cit., pp. 481-84; McKeachie, op. cit., pp. 1125-48.

[70]Reece, op. cit., p. 130; Metcalf et al., op. cit., pp. 51-52.

[71]V. L. Coughlin, "Improving Library School Teaching," *Library Education: An International Survey*, op. cit., p. 314.

4

LIBRARY-CENTERED LIBRARY EDUCATION

INTRODUCTION

The emphasis upon theory in library education over the decades since Williamson represents a headlong flight from the simplistic economies of Melvil Dewey if not a repudiation of the philosophy of John Dewey. Opportunities to observe and experience the workings of the real world of library service in schools that minimize the practical component have been modest indeed. More often than not, they have been tacitly understood to happen on the students' own time. Generally they have been systematic or casual, depending upon the proclivities of the individual instructor. Experience in library operations could be assured only if the student were a part-time employee, but in this experience the elements of control and supervision are removed from the educational function. Practical knowledge concurrent with classroom theory has been largely adventitious rather than orchestrated. Yet what school or department in a university's applied sciences complex would allow a student passage through the curriculum without the marriage of hand and eye to the test tube, mineral matter, fetal pig or other instrumentality of the trade?

Lukenbill equates "experiential learning" with "laboratory learning" and finds that there are underlying philosophical assumptions for its justification: "That one learns by doing; that learning through real experience engages the learner's mind, emotions, and whole being; that no artificial barrier, such as memorization for future actions, interferes with the 'here and now' experience; and most importantly, that reflection on the experience is necessary for true learning as it allows the learner to generalize and intellectualize about the phenomena which have just been experienced."[1] But to offer the student this chance to reflect upon that which has "just" been experienced requires a structure in which the taxonomies discussed reveal a seminar-laboratory pedagogy. What, however, is the laboratory to be? In the following pages some ideas involving the laboratory as macrocosm and the laboratory as microcosm will be examined, for these constructs have not been given the attention they deserve. Perhaps we ought to proceed with care and humility at this stage in our explorations. Peters noted that "contingencies abound when such a concrete level of the implementation of general principles is reached. About such contingencies there is very little, philosophically speaking, to say. . . . Philosophy is only one component in educational theory. . . . Philosophy contributes to practical wisdom but is not a substitute for it."[2]   The search for a "reality base" in a curriculum in which theory is enshrined is a hazardous enterprise and exemplifies the conditional nature of the teaching-learning process.

THE LIBRARY-CENTERED LIBRARY SCHOOL

In a conference paper, Patricia B. Knapp, whose distinguished work at Monteith College had gained wide interest in library education, raised important questions about the nature of the literature of librarianship, the structure of library science, and the application of the discovery method to library education. She began her presentation by examining the shibboleth, spoken at commencements, that "the library is the heart of the college," and suggested that it is largely myth. At best it is real for only 15 percent of undergraduate students; at worst it is a meaningless phrase in the educational lexicon, unctuously uttered by florid-faced college presidents. Assuming, however, that learning through the library is "consistent with recognized objectives of liberal education and with widely accepted learning theory," she offered a parallel case for library-centered library education. Knapp defined this kind of education as "a teaching method in which library school students find it necessary to use the library as a systematically organized body of resources, i.e., to find materials not assigned or recommended by their instructors." In Knapp's judgment, the case for library-centered library education was self-evident: librarians will be working in libraries, and they must master certain principles and skills that can be achieved only through use of the organization of the library. Specifically, what do students need to learn about libraries, how much should they learn before they assume their first professional position, and how are they to learn? she suggested that "the arguments used to support library-centered teaching at the undergraduate level may help us clarify our specific objectives and methods."[3]

It is important to point out that Knapp did not insist on a total learning experience in library education through a library-centered method: "Whenever learning objectives can be most effectively achieved through textbooks, required readings on reserve, distributed bibliographies or other such guidance from the instructor, these methods should be used." But she did insist that a viable curriculum in library and information science is a pedagogical contradiction if it does not include objectives that can be achieved with a library (or other information center) at the core of the learning process.[4]

Bruner indicated that "the curriculum of a subject should be determined by the most fundamental understanding that can be achieved of the underlying principles that give structure to that subject."[5] If, as Knapp argued, library and bibliographic organization reflect, "imperfectly to be sure, but recognizably," the structures of the several disciplines, then "experience in the use of this organization is an appropriate method for acquiring understanding of this structure." Add to the importance of discerning structure the use of the library as a tool in which students can discover "at least some semblance of the structure of knowledge," and one arrives at a learning method consistent with sound educational theory.[6]

Moreover, if this is acceptable in theory and practicable in method for undergraduate education, how much more desirable might it be for library education itself? Knapp attempted to answer this rhetorical question by analyzing the specific objectives she posed for library-centered library education.

The Content of Library-Centered Library Education

Because librarians embrace the universe of recorded knowledge, "it is almost impossible to define the boundaries of the literature of the field." However, it is necessary to assay a definition, because to do so is a precondition for determining "the kind and degree of mastery we expect our students to attain."

On the other hand, "content" may be described as "the literature produced by and for the library profession." Similar to other professions, librarianship is equipped with primary and secondary materials to facilitate the transfer of information. Librarianship has books and professional journals; monographs and "state-of-the-art" reviews; indexing and abstracting services; dictionaries and encyclopedias; biographical and institutional directories; yearbooks; statistical compilations; textbooks and histories; annual reports; handbooks and manuals; and other professional "tools." Knapp called these sources "the literature related to the practice of librarianship" and distinguished between a "specialized body of knowledge" (which is a characteristic of all professions) and its application in practice.

Thus narrowly defined, Knapp indicated that "no one would quarrel with mastery of the literature of professional librarianship . . . as an appropriate objective of library education." But the degree of mastery, which presumably separates the core curriculum from the specialized areas, is questionable. It is general practice not to have the student whose declared goal is school librarianship "master" the professional literature of university or medical librarianship. Decisions of this sort are based usually on consideration of time rather than pedagogy, but they must be explicit in curricular statements of aims and objectives.

A greater educational concern arises if the definition of "content" includes "the body of knowledge upon which librarianship is based." But this corpus, the literature librarians work with, includes everything and reduces to absurdity the possibility of mastering a body of knowledge so defined.

Even in subject specialization total mastery becomes a pious abstraction rather than a discernible educational goal. Some measure of acquaintance, therefore, is acceptable for the student prior to his assumption of professional responsibility.

As a means of escaping the illogical pursuit of "content" Knapp suggested "the development of some sort of structural conception of the organization of communication records in society. Perhaps it might be thought of as a special kind of language, the language of bibliographic organization. . . . Our students, then, would be expected to master not all the literatures librarians work with, but a language or set of languages for communicating with them." In the "ill-defined field" of librarianship, Knapp declared that epistemological considerations loom significant.[7]

Library-Centered Teaching Methods

Traditional methods of instruction (as analyzed and discussed in the preceding chapter), in more or less degree, employ the services of a library, if only to have the student check out a book on reserve. As students progress in their program, it is assumed that they will have more and more occasion "to use library organization to find resources not assigned or recommended by their instructors." But Knapp found no evidence that "library school students use a wide range of library resources, use the literature of library science in depth, [or] use library organization itself to a considerable extent in connection with the term papers, the reference exercises, the annotated bibliographies, and the examinations commonly employed in library science programs." Her general impression was that when students "go beyond" suggested assignments which require acquaintance with the organization of the library, they do so because they are "unable to locate (or borrow for home use) the titles recommended. In other words, much of library science students' use of the organization of the library occurs by default." Knapp opined that this kind of library use "produces not a grasp of bibliographical organization, but rather a desperate acceptance of the value of library scrounging."

Although Knapp did not equate discovery with serendipity, she rejected the idea of "coverage" of materials, which is a content-oriented concept, for a systematic "discovery-through-the-library method of teaching" within a "structure-of-the-discipline framework." Not only is this approach a more powerful method for initiative and disciplined freedom than the examination of long lists of sources, as in reference or bibliography, but it is superior to "the case method, in which [the student] is likely to spend more time on amateur psychologizing but acquire no better understanding of the intricate and complex relationship among the sources of information and ideas to be found in the library."

Because setting the boundaries of "library literature is problematic no matter how we define it," Knapp averred that mastery of the literature "in the old-fashioned sense of knowing content is probably an unobtainable and possibly an undesirable objective of professional education in a field which is changing so fast." Library-centered assignments, which emphasize the organization of knowledge and the structure of disciplines, "can help students acquire a conceptual framework, a theoretical foundation for a continuing process of learning."[8]

Knapp and the Teaching-Learning Process

In her Monteith College library-centered experiment, Knapp formulated what she called the "Idea of the Way." The "Way" was a theoretical justification for college instruction in the use of the library that centered on "the intellectual processes involved in retrieval of information and ideas from the highly complex system our society uses to organize its stored records." To avoid the terminology of "the documentalists, the information theorists," she settled on the simple metaphor of the "Way" as implying both "path" and "method," that is, a "path-way." The focus was on the students finding a path, starting from their own resources, their intellectual equipment, and proceeding "to where you want to go (your purpose)." The "Way" as a method involved an apprehension of library organization and the tools "of scholarly communication." The ideal-typical pathway, then, would lead to a goal where tools and organization revealed an understanding of both, a congruence of the apparatus of knowledge and the network of library organization by which it is transferred from producer to user. In planning sequences for this endeavor, Knapp established four criteria: "1. The sequence must have intrinsic unity and coherence; 2. The total program must be functionally related to the curriculum; 3. Every assignment must have genuine intellectual content; 4. Every assignment must be practical, that is, it must not require extraordinary library services or resources."[9]

The results of her undergraduate experiment, Knapp assumed, could be incorporated into the library science curriculum. One such concept would be a discovery of the organizational limitations of libraries. At some point in the process, the student should gain sight of the fact that the structure of knowledge revealed by traditional library organization may not be a mirror image of the cognitive structure in which learning experiences most felicitously occur. She cited as principles implicit behavioral traits in the seasoned librarian which would be regarded as revelations for the beginning student: 1) bibliographic tools like the card catalog "are relatively inefficient for dealing with large and abstract ideas"; 2) "the more voluminous literature there is on a given subject, the less necessary it is to use the bibliographic machinery which controls that literature"; 3) "bibliographic organization of scholarship is different from library organization" because the latter reflects discipline, concept and method whereas the former emphasizes subject and form; 4) most scholarly disciplines do not depend on the library for their primary needs.[10]

But an emphasis on the virtues of articulating structure and providing heuristic experiences may reveal a pedagogical dilemma: "If we identify and make explicit the general principles which underlie the structure of librarianship and use these as organizing principles in library education, will we deny our students the power and joy of discovering such principles for themselves?" Knapp was not sure how this paradox could best be resolved, save to suggest that the answer resides in "teaching style," by which she meant a mode of instruction that creates the conditions conducive to resolution of the dilemma. She was less vague, however, on instructional methods *unfit* for realizing this goal: "The expository mode of teaching, whether the exposition be concerned with conveying discrete pieces of information or with the enunciation of general principles, will not produce the kind of librarians we want." For Knapp the *summum bonum* in library education is that "it be permeated with the excitement of discovering fundamental structure in the chaotic world of books and ideas." And the vehicle for achieving this end is a library-centered learning sequence facilitating discovery through process and structure.[11]

THE LIBRARY SCHOOL LIBRARY AS LABORATORY

In a learning sequence for which the library is the center of instructional activity, the limitations of *ex cathedra* methods of transmitting knowledge can be avoided. Moreover, an exploration of the organization of knowledge and the structure of disciplined thought provides for the student a process that is epiphanic rather than didactic. But the university—or college—library is for the prospective librarian a macrocosm, the real world, and as such cannot wholly be the locus for the educational control of planned activities. Of the three categories of content-centered professional activity, the first—"the literature produced by and for the library profession"—appears amenable to the pedagogical enterprise, that is, to definition, delimitation, and systematic analysis. The logical unit for this endeavor is the library school library where this literature is housed. Implicit in Knapp's analysis of library-centered library education is the concept of a specialized library which could function as the locus of the teaching-learning process.[12]

Imagine, if you will, the ideal library science library, a splendid and substantial collection of monographs, periodicals, microforms, indexes and other bibliographic sources, A-V materials, an OCLC terminal, an online computerized retrieval component, an automated circulation system—in short, all of the print and nonprint materials and the concomitant hardware necessary to support the instructional program. With such a unit, Knapp's initial category, the "organizational and functional context in which [librarianship] is practiced," could be harnessed to the educational enterprise.

One would surmise that the uses of a library science collection in some educational venture as a logical extension of Knapp's theories about library-centered library education would have merited some attention among theoreticians of library education. Alas, this is not the case. When I undertook a search of the relevant literature I was confident of finding exemplary information on the relationship between this special library unit and the instructional process. I shared Kaser's astonishment at the paucity of material available: "A search of the literature reveals very little information concerning the libraries of the library schools."[13]

Kaser's remarks appeared in a 1964 issue of the *Journal of Education for Librarianship* devoted to quarters and equipment for library schools. In preparing their articles for this issue, library educators discovered how meager was information on any aspect of library science libraries but especially on the pedagogical connection.

In a 1949 Unesco study, Danton alluded to an independent library science collection, but emphasized the importance of the school's being in proximity to "a university or other large library," not only for bibliographic and reference resources, but also for the resources Knapp called "the body of knowledge upon which librarianship is based."[14] Following Danton, little appeared in the literature directly or indirectly concerned with the educational implications of library school collections until the 1964 issue of *Journal of Education for Librarianship*.

Monroe's discussion of facilities and quarters in that issue reinforced Danton's concern with proximity to the larger library but added two other desiderata fundamental to activities in library education: availability of "laboratory collections" and "of library materials of all types for analysis in the classroom as well as at the student's desk." Although laboratory materials for study in a special collection or in a classroom may create problems in cost and design, Monroe considered these facilities an integral part of library education. Noting that "professional preparation required mastery of fact and detail as well as the mastery of principles . . . and exercise of judgment," she considered practice materials crucial to the educative process. In order to apply library principles to particular materials, "the library school professional library . . . must provide a model in sound university and special librarianship." By this, Monroe did not mean a collection that "looks good" and merely projects a favorable "image," but a working library where "organization and service are related to the school's demands, and the close contact with faculty activities makes possible serving the research as well as instructional purposes of graduate library education."[15]

Other contributors to this special issue of *JEL*, in their discussions of ventilation and lavatories, rarely commented upon the instructional program as it might relate to the library collection. Where the resources were to be employed as a "laboratory" function, they were mentioned most often in connection with courses in cataloging and classification, and the library was thought of as a "reading room book collection."[16] One contributor noted that a seminar laboratory, where most courses took place, had served as a classroom, study hall, "home-room" for coats and umbrellas, and "a regular library collection repository." Fortunately at the time of writing the hapless situation was being repaired.[17]

The absence of clear educational objectives in the employment of library school collections confirmed Kaser's judgment of the professional picture: there seemed "little, if any, consensus among library educators as to what they feel a library school collection must do for their students."[18] Although this may reflect a healthy diversity in philosophy of library education, Monroe expressed a less sanguine view. Any discussion of the place of the library collection in the overall design of quarters depends on answering the question, "What is library education?" To Monroe it seemed obvious "that since we do not know what library education is or should be, we have no agreed-upon basis for designing library school quarters."[19]

Two years later, Brian Land, writing in *JEL*, considered the relationship of facilities to educational objectives with a precision lacking in earlier accounts. The question of quarters separate from or integrated with a university library was raised. Land favored the former, since the university library perceives the library school as an "expansion joint," a unit that can be moved out when a space emergency arises (this monstrous perception may seem bizarre, but I am personally familiar with a situation in which a library school existed at the sufferance of the university library for several years). A separate location removes this threat and gives a school an identity it otherwise would not enjoy. Although proximity to larger resources remains important, separate facilities were seen by Land as an ideal.

From a separate facility the idea of a separate, self-contained collection follows logically: "The library school library which is well-stocked, attractively furnished, and up-to-date in its equipment and methods, can provide the student with a first-hand opportunity to see the embodiment of the ideas and ideals proclaimed in the classroom. The library school library, therefore, should be a model library." Land used the word "model" in the sense Monroe suggested: a full, working unit capable of sustaining the instructional mission of the school. Land favorably quoted Osborn that the collection not merely be a reading room for students but "strive to simulate actual library conditions."

The ideal Land described is still a traditional ideal in the sense that the collection itself is not perceived as a laboratory for learning so much as a perfectly run system, without infelicities, where students can discern what a library should be rather than what libraries all too often are. Indeed, the "laboratory" function for classification, cataloging and bibliography would be adjacent to the library where students would be able to practice routines. Incredible as it may seem, one of the routines suggested was the typing of catalog cards "according to accepted bibliographical format and style."[20]

Downs agreed with Land as to the value of a separate library science collection located in or near a larger library. With the resources of the main library at hand, it follows that "no attempt should be made . . . for a self-sufficient book collection in the library school library. The primary aim should be to provide a strong, well-selected, up-to-date assemblage of books, journals, pamphlets, slides, and films, but to relegate to the general library collection out-dated, little-used materials, such as earlier editions of books, older files of periodicals, individual library reports, and most foreign-language publications."[21]

Lieberman, like the others who have contributed to the discussion of facilities, pointed out the necessity for utilizing technological innovations in library education. The purpose of technology harnessed to an educational program should be "to devise a wider range of means of getting effective student learning," to modify or invigorate "the old traditions of the teacher-student relationship, the rigid methodology of lecture, recitation, laboratory work and the term paper, and the narrow conception of human learning as specific conditioning."[22] Whatever the emphases, a common theme in these commentaries was that the library school should be far more than a poor cousin of the university library, occupying borrowed space and existing in fear of eviction.

Stevens suggested that university library administrators favor a library science library in order to avoid demands by inept students and faculties of library schools on the resources of the main collection. Ghettoization of library science facilities would serve to reduce the animosity that pervades relationships between university librarians and library school students and faculties.[23] Although not explicitly critical of this relationship, it is interesting to note that both Land and Lee cited as the major advantage of a separate collection "fast access to books essential to student needs" and the avoidance of "having library school students monopolize books and seats in the main library."[24]

A few studies have focused upon the techniques of furnishing library science libraries. Niederhauser[25] and Wetmore[26] emphasized routines for control of materials, while Truax[27] considered collection building as well as design esthetics. In a report on the status of professionals in charge of library school collections, it was suggested that the low profile accorded the library school librarian was due to the indifference of library school deans to the potential of the libraries as vital centers in the instructional setting: "One can compare the status of law or medical librarians . . . as well as the physical facilities available to librarians in medical or law schools, and he will discover that there is something wrong with our profession and our library schools."[28]

Typical of the indifference or antipathy to any suggestion about the use of the library school library in a creative, educational way is the thoughtful proposal by Fingerson and the equally thoughtless rejoinder by Lanier. The former advocated the concept of the self-contained library school collection in order to provide students with "primary library experience," increased opportunities for "research and systems study and design," and the inter-relationship of systems such as acquisitions, administration, cataloging, serials, and reference, and "familiarity training in clerical skills." Library school students, Fingerson averred, "require a learning environment where they can put classroom theories into actual employment prior to graduation."[29] The only reply to this reasoned suggestion was a letter accusing the author of advocating "not education for librarianship but technical training." Such training, it was argued, "is best reserved for internships and on the job assignments."[30]

These fragments from the literature, with few exceptions, demonstrate the virtual absence of any attempt at elevated discourse on the possibilities of the library shcool library in the teaching-learning process. While it may be that the idea will not, ultimately, withstand the rigors of analytic refutation, no theoretical objections have been adduced to dismiss its potential in the resolution of the theory-practice conundrum.

Theoretical Justification

If library-centered learning employing the resources of the library school library is worthy of trial, it must satisfy criteria legitimized by studies in educational theory and sound curricular methods. For our purposes that would mean fidelity to the Dubin-Taveggia modes, the Reeceian taxonomy, and the dicta for a resolution of theory and practice suggested by McGrath. One way in which these constructs could be applied would be to utilize the collection primarily as a vehicle for the reconciliation of principles and skills, with emphasis upon the ultimate identification of the former by application to actual problems in need of solution. The mode of inquiry thus defined would not preclude gaining some expertise in process, but discrete tasks, in McGrath's words, that might "cultivate the essential skills" would be performed only to the extent of illuminating "the principles involved . . . but not so much as to make of learning a profitless repetitive exercise." The kind of experience would offer opportunities to discover larger meanings arising from specific conditions. The extent could be controlled by defining the purpose of the learning experience to preclude carrying discrete tasks beyond student apprehension of their underlying principles. The temporal arrangement satisfies the concept of "concurrence" in professional education in lieu of a deferred experience, the common characteristic of internship programs.[31] Finally, the spatial criterion is obvious. A library school collection affords the propinquity necessary to impose systematic control over the environment in which the learning and teaching take place.

Library-centered learning in the macrocosm of the university library, however epiphanic and heuristic, would ignore the warning of Williamson and Reece. The former cautioned against a total recreation of "reality" for that could easily result in a "purely incidental" absorption of principles.[32] The latter noted that order, system, control and effective expenditure of time could best be achieved in a learning situation which perforce involved strategies that fell short of real events.[33] For both educators unqualified allegiance to a non-simulated learning situation missed the point of professional education entirely.

The combination of seminar with laboratory creates a mode of instruction consistent with a judicious balance of the teaching and learning component in the process. Face-to-face instruction permits the element of teaching guidance to complement a form of independent study where student initiative can determine the success or failure of self-appropriated learning. Moreover, the defined and delimited locus of inquiry permits control over the educative process not possible in a host library removed from the instructional milieu.[34] The question, *Where?*, to accompany McGrath's criteria could thus be satisfactorily answered.

That which Knapp regarded as axiomatic, a library-centered library education, should obtain in the microcosm as well as the larger reality of the university library. By definition, situations worthy of study exist in a library school library; "the literature produced by and for the library profession" is housed in such a way as to permit systematic observation of structure. That is, the materials represent an ordered organization of specialized recorded knowledge.

It remains for us to examine the learning and teaching strategies that inhere in the "seminar-laboratory" mode of instruction. For when this kind of educational activity is pursued, the student must abandon his role as passive receptacle, and the teacher must eschew his traditional authoritarian approach. Both student and instructor will find these departures from tradition difficult at first, and perhaps more demanding throughout the entire process. But the rewards for both are potentially greater. I am persuaded that, given an atmosphere under which new conditions of learning can prosper, students will in their explorations embody the general features of a reflective experience that pervade the philosophical writings of John Dewey.[35]

LEARNING STRATEGIES IN LIBRARY-CENTERED
LIBRARY EDUCATION

In a "seminar-laboratory" course in which theory might be reconciled to experience, the emphasis is on student learning rather than *ex cathedra* authority. The willingness on the part of the faculty to enlist students in the creation of their own learning experiences is Rogerian and not particularly unusual. "I have come to feel," Carl Rogers said, "that the only learning which significantly influences behavior is self-discovered, self-appropriated learning."[36] Martell set forth criteria for what he called "student-centered teaching" for creative learning: "Student-centered teaching results when students are allowed (1) to set classroom objectives, (2) to establish means of arriving at these objectives, and (3) to evaluate progress toward attainment of these objectives."[37] The objectives of participatory education are, in theory, an improvement in classroom performance and an increase in motivation.

Although traditional methods of teaching persist, there has been no paucity of voices calling for an end to, or at least a departure from, the "traditionally authoritarian pattern of much teaching and learning" which precludes student involvement. Thus Morison noted that:

> Ever since the student started kindergarten he has felt the need to fulfill the expectations of his teachers. This pattern is so fixed that even if the university encouraged a more adult attitude the student might find it difficult to readjust. Unfortunately in too many instances the university merely perpetuates the old pattern and rewards the student for fulfilling the expectations set forth in prescribed reading lists, course credits and set curricula. Thus the student remains in his passive receptive state and hesitates to take command of himself.[38]

But this very freedom of students to create their own learning experiences and the concomitant refusal of faculty to erect didactic structures often cause panic reactions. Students have become so immured in the prison of traditional, authoritarian instructional methods that they fear the very freedom they imagined to be desirable. In any curricular experiment involving a shift from traditional modes of presentation to student-centered learning, the fears of students must be allayed before significant learning experiences can be won. Library-centered library education, whether the locus is the university library or the library collection as laboratory, lends itself to student initiative, but the student must disenthrall himself from the anxieties that the very process of liberation engenders.

Where students seek out problems and tasks in a library-centered library educational experience, they should be equipped with techniques which will facilitate their power to observe and draw generalizations from specific units of activity. Following are some of the techniques and strategies that may be applied to the practical component of library-centered library education.

Critical Incident Theory

In her Monteith College Library studies, Knapp asked her students to keep a record, or log, of their search strategy in library-centered assignments. Her aim in utilizing this technique was twofold: "It was hoped that these reports would provide useful information about what students experience when they know little or nothing about the topic on which they seek information. But, more important, it was hoped that the reports would heighten the student's own awareness of the thinking processes involved in his search."[39]

But despite her careful attention to an explanation of keeping the log and recording the search process, "the log did not prove to be a good teaching device." She found no evidence that it helped students perceive the search patterns they were using or might better have used. It was, moreover, complex and time-consuming. Students varied in their interpretation of the directions for recording the steps they took. Thus it did not lend itself to detailed analysis of the students' search processes."[40]

Despite Knapp's negative conclusion, some kind of recording procedure, in conjunction with insights gleaned from the relatively small but growing body of critical incident theory, seems too promising to ignore. Although the "critical incident" or "critical requirements" technique has been traced back to secretarial studies in the 1920s,[41] elaborate use of the method was first carried out by John C. Flanagan and his associates in defining fighter pilot effectiveness during World War II. In 1954, Flanagan published a seminal state-of-the-art paper on the technique.[42] Shortly thereafter it was being tentatively explored as a method useful to categories of the educative process.[43] When applied to teaching and learning, modifications are necessary because, as Good pointed out, "the technique was originally intended to study men at work on machines (including airplanes, scientific instruments, and assembly lines), whereas in the field of education men are studied as they work with men, involving human interaction and a number of variables."[44]

Researchers have largely used critical incident method in collecting data for categories of teaching effectiveness, but little attention has been paid to the technique as a means of constructing categories of learning effectiveness. Reluctance to assign students a responsible role in the technique has been based, understandably, upon their age and lack of sophistication. Yet in at least one study, teachers had students in grade levels five through eleven contribute critical incidents, and analysis of the data resulted in a verdict of cautious optimism.[45] Indeed, Flanagan and Jung reported that in curricular experiments which emphasized student responsibility for initiating learning sequences, data on critical incident collecting have proven, when monitored by the teacher, of considerable value and accuracy.[46] Biddle's review of empirical studies of classroom interaction suggested ways of conceptualizing designs by which the teaching and learning processes can both be accommodated to this technique. In the literature of critical incident studies two types of observational entities have been distinguished and described, phenomenal units and analytic units.

Phenomenal units have been defined as "natural breaks in the stream of classroom processes that may reasonably be assumed to be recognized by classroom participants."[47] Given different names by different investigators (segments, episodes), the units signify a discrete activity or task, in a sequence of activities exhibiting a direction, that points toward an outcome as yet largely undefined.[48] Phenomenal units are characterized by objective description of the activity; raw datum is recorded and, at the moment of notation, unanalyzed.

Analytic units "vary in size and reflect various conceptual assumptions." Moreover, they "may or may not be recognized as 'natural' units of classroom discourse by participants; normally they are discussed in abstract terminology that has meaning mainly to the investigators." Interpreting analytic units has been called a *strategy*, "a set of verbal actions that serves to attain certain results and to guard against others," or a *venture*, "a segment of discourse consisting of a set of utterances dealing with a single topic and having a single over-arching content objective."

Phenomenal units are peculiarly the province of a student's inquiry in his sequence of responses to an indeterminate situation. Analytic units, on the other hand, "reflect the sophisticated concerns of the investigator rather than those of the participant," singularly a function of the teaching process.[49] A vehicle for a coherent teaching-learning procedure appears to reside in the complementary aspect of both constructs. The structure of the seminar-laboratory mode of instruction, I am persuaded, can provide a framework for utilizing some form of critical incident technique, with the log, or record, containing the recorded phenomena to be analyzed in the milieu of seminar interaction.

Let us examine how this technique might serve to apprehend theory from a series of discrete observations. To serve the purposes of the "laboratory" component of the seminar-laboratory mode, it is probably necessary to modify the insights of critical incident technique in one important respect. The problem inherent in critical incident studies where, as Mayhew points out, success or lack thereof remains undefined during the process, is the lack of confidence in the "criticalness" of the phenomenal units. That is, the phenomenal units at some point prior to the normal completion of a sequence of laboratory tasks ought to reveal, through seminar analysis, a resolution of inquiry. Merely an additive procedure of effective and ineffective incidents is not sufficient to culminate in that moment of discovery where principles can be apprehended simply by arithmetical fiat.

The analytic units to be effective would have to emerge a posteriori so that the critical incident (or cluster of incidents that cohered in uniform connections) was made manifest. This crucial incident would then be recognized as the conclusion of the phenomenal process and as the signifying element in perceiving the larger reference. The critical incident, in other words, would represent the unifying point at which the student could cease practical tasks, the latter having served the purpose of an incipient illumination of principle. McGrath's temporal criterion could then be said to have been satisfied; so too the Reeceian emphasis upon economy of time as the raison d' être of professional training.

Mayhew suggested that the significance of critical incident technique "lies chiefly in providing empirically derived classifications of behavior which can then be used either as a framework for subsequent measurement or as the material out of which evaluation instruments can be developed." Moreover, he stated that various situations involving problem-solving, incidents of effective or ineffective thinking, in short, "categories of cognitive behavior," are amenable to critical incident methods."[50] For library-centered library education utilizing the library science library as the foundational unit of the teaching-learning process, a variation of critical incident technique could serve as a vehicle that would assist, in Dewey's words, in the "transformation of an indeterminate situation into one that is so determinate in its constituent distinctions and relations as to convert the elements of the original situation into a unified whole."[51]

Dewey's Inquiry Model

Another learning strategy in student-centered instruction using the broader framework of library-centered library education is the employment of a model of inquiry based upon John Dewey's famous analysis of sequential learning in *How We Think*. this is not to suggest that a slavish adherence to the precise sequence is necessary or even desirable. Indeed, Dewey himself warned against such literalism:

> The disciplined or logically trained mind—the aim of the educative process—is the mind able to judge how far each of these steps needs to be carried in any particular situation. No cast-iron rules can be laid down. Each case has to be dealt with as it arises, on the basis of its importance and of the context in which it occurs. To take too much pains in one case is as foolish—as illogical—as to take too little in another. . . . The trained mind is the one that best grasps the degree of

observation, forming of ideas, reasoning, and experimental testing required in any special case. . . . What is important is that the mind should be sensitive to problems and skilled in methods of attack and solution.[52]

When students pursue self-appropriated areas of inquiry in the "laboratory" that is the library science library, they respond to situations that, in Dewey's words, indicate a "felt difficulty." The logical process follows with the "locating and defining" of the problem which caused the felt difficulty. At this point seminar interaction may be useful in articulating the problem, developing suggestions toward possible solutions, guidance (preferably nondirective and unobtrusive) from the teacher, and discussion among students themselves. At this point, too, the assignment of practical tasks and the log for recording phenomenal units enter the learning strategy.

The step that Dewey called "reasoning" is a matter of translating discrete data into meaningful patterns. As the student accumulates a mass of critical data, as more intimate and extensive observation occurs, a refined procedure for accepting and discarding conjecture takes place. Although this process can be frustrating, persistence is rewarded with information that moves the student toward the development of ideas that might resolve discrepancies. At this stage the student is seeking consciously among the phenomena observed a unifying configuration, a condition favorable to "some hypothetically entertained conclusion."[53] At a point when a congeries of ideas, based upon analysis of phenomenal units, suggests the critical incident, the student is able with a degree of confidence to abandon the practical task and begin those advanced processes that will lead to an illumination of principles applicable to the macrocosm.

Polanyi and others have argued that graduate students are often presented a "false ideal" of research and learning as a thoroughly reasonable, logical and orderly enterprise, whereas in reality it is "sometimes intuitive and often messy."[54] The inquiry model as described above may give the impression of aseptic purity; of course no inquiry process can be tidy. However, even allowing for the disorderliness that characterizes inquiry, the Deweyan model may serve ably for this particular kind of learning.

What we are trying to assay in these pages is the merit that might inhere in a method of library-centered instruction using the library collection as a microcosm for practical tasks. The mode as presented is designed to incorporate a *controlled way* of reconciling theory and skills in the curriculum. The author's hope is that the method avoids the perennial criticism of internships and other extramural work contacts while it combines the most fruitful modes of instruction by eschewing the least desirable didactic structures.

TEACHING STRATEGIES IN LIBRARY-CENTERED LIBRARY EDUCATION

Pity the poor professor of graduate library education. This overworked wretch must teach six to nine hours a week, publish one or two five-page articles a year, and suffer the indignity of only 22 weeks of vacation per annum. Little wonder that he is too exhausted to engage the student in anything more than the traditional lecture method of transmitting information. For if students are asked to cast aside their role as passive vessels in experiential learning tasks, faculty too must abandon the jejune and unimaginative instructional modes to which they have become habituated. What follows is an examination of a few of the possible techniques that have been discussed in the education literature, strategies that permit both research and evaluation of the teaching role itself and a vehicle for non-traditional instruction.

Action Research

The investigation of untried assumptions in library-centered library education cannot perforce be observed, examined and analyzed in the manner of a formal, controlled but artificial laboratory experiment. Attention to the problems peculiar to this kind of student-centered learning has been focused on conditions where a number of relatively complex variables are forever interacting. Waples and Tyler used the term "service study" to characterize a "method of investigation that is more systematic than ordinary thinking but far less systematic and carefully controlled than the research study."[55] Whitney classed this type of "descriptive research" in the category of "case-group investigations," in which "more or less unitary social or academic groups are isolated for analysis, usually with the purpose of possible improvement."[56] Because investigations of this nature are universally apposite to the uncertainties of the teaching-learning process, refinements in method have become a considered, ongoing enterprise.

A significant contribution to the adaptation of research procedures appropriate to this analysis was made by Corey in 1953, who popularized the term " action research." Although antecedents of this kind of investigatory process can be traced to Dewey,[57] the procedure had rarely been exploited. Caswell noted that:

> Educational research over the years has rather extensively adopted the concepts of procedure developed in the physical sciences. As a consequence, the laboratory-controlled situation has been the ideal widely sought. Thus research has tended to be rather far removed from the daily activities of the classroom teacher, the supervisor, and the school principal. The view has been gaining acceptance that this condition is an unsound one.[58]

Corey defined action research as "the process by which practitioners attempt to study their problems scientifically in order to guide, correct and evaluate their decisions and actions."[59] Major emphases in action research, according to Good, include 1) a "developmental design, with the hypothesis and method subject to modification during the course of the action program, and with due consideration of all interdependent groups concerned in any changes to be made," and 2) a "determination of the value of the action project in terms of the extent to which methods and findings make possible improvement in practice in a particular situation and realization of social and educational purposes."[60] That is, because applications are not always manifest in the formulation of a scientific principle, the practitioner finds onerous the "task of translating into an actual classroom program the outcomes of pure research derived under conditions of strict control."[61] thus, a primary purpose of action research is the "integration of study (theory) with action (implementation)."[62] One of the most attractive features of action research is its flexibility, the opportunities to modify the method during the time span of the activity, the refreshing admission that in the world of educational research, subjects cannot be analyzed like billiard balls, for if anything aptly characterizes student heuristics in a library-centered environment it is the element of uncertainty.

Participant Observation

If action research is a method which contributes to the teacher's functional knowledge of the phenomena with which he must cope, participant observation is a logical activity in the analyzing and examining process. It is important at the outset to face the chief problem in participant observation, that of possible distortion, because the very nature of action research in curricular experimentation precludes non-participant observation. The latter would negate the interactive dynamic, which contributes to the education of both student and instructor in the teaching-learning process. But there are varying degrees of detachment and involvement permissible in participant observation; it is in the technique of the dual role that the problem of projective distortion becomes significant or relatively harmless.

Indeed, it is not possible to observe without participating and achieve an unbiased measure: "Such distortion is not restricted to the social sciences; a similar phenomenon may be observed in physics, where, for instance, the apparatus used to detect the behavior of particles in atomic radiation actually distorts the movement of these particles (the Heisenberg effect)."[63] In social anthropology the value of participant observation has long been recognized. Morris and Charlotte Schwartz defend the technique, when the involvement is identified and qualified in the interpretation of the results:

The issue is not whether the participant observer will become . . . involved, but rather the nature of the involvement. The involvement, whether it is closer to one end of the continuum (sympathetic identification) or the other end (projective distortion), is very little a function of an observer's role. Rather, it is primarily a function of his experience, awareness, and personality constellation and the way these become integrated with a particular situation. . . . Sympathetic identification includes empathic communication and imaginative participation in the life of the observed through identification and role taking. In this type of involvement the observer is both detached and affectively participating; he feels no need to moralize or judge the interacting; his attitude is one of interested curiosity and matter-of-fact inquiry directed toward understanding the observed.[64]

Common sense tells us that the role of any conscientious teacher in almost every formal learning situation consists precisely of that continual activity which ranges between sympathetic identification and unobtrusive observation. Those educational experiments wherein the dialectic is conducted behind the researcher's one-way screen or hidden microphone, whether they are useful or ludicrous, serve no purpose in these discussions. Educators have recognized and accepted the values that inhere in participant observation, particularly for studies which cannot be isolated without constructing artificial barriers to normal classroom behavior. Good cited several advantages to be gained in participant observation:

1. The participant observer is not basically limited by prejudgment, but can reformulate the problem as he goes along.

2. Closer contact with the situation enables the participant observer to avoid misleading or meaningless responses.

3. The participant observer can continually remodify his categories to provide sharper analysis of problems under study.

4. The participant observer may absorb considerable information which may seem at the time irrelevant, but later may prove valuable for perspective.

5. On the scene, the participant observer can move more easily back and forth between data gathering and desk analysis.

6. Through free data gathering, the participant observer distorts less the difficult-to-quantify aspects of a problem.

7. The participant observer can select later subjects in such a way as to throw additional light on emerging hypotheses.[65]

Because the appropriate conditions for action research and participant observation usually arise out of   "an urgent practical or felt need, with a goal of application of results and improvement of practice in the particular setting where the group or investigator works, through processes of group planning, execution, and evaluation,"[66]   the techniques of both would appear to serve the teaching function in library-centered library education well, and provide the environment for a conjunction of theory and experience.

The Inquiry Model and Critical Incident

Library-centered library education requires a reversal of the philosophy of theory and practice in traditional, class presentation modes of instruction. The latter employs the didactic method of transmitting theory and leaving its application to a future practical situation. Dewey's model of the process of inquiry, however, holds that the illumination of principles can be the end result of a process whose origins lie in the "felt difficulty" of a practical problem. Accordingly, teaching activities in this mode are defined, in part, by the learners' responses and reactions to the practical difficulty.

Where the initial response to a felt difficulty is one of frustration or doubt or curiosity, the teacher can provide corroboration, reinforcement, and assurances of legitimacy. Validation of the student's feelings of perplexity is important as therapy as well as sound pedagogy. As the student's felt difficulty is articulated, the teacher can assist in defining and delimiting the activity it would involve. In the difficult and often frustrating attempts to make sense of the discrete phenomenal units recorded, the teacher assumes the analytic function. This can be accomplished in the interaction of the seminar meetings. As the student attempts to develop analytic units from the phenomenal data, the teacher's role is one of guidance toward critical incident configuration. The identification *with the student* of *the* critical incident is the crucial contribution of the teacher, for it signifies the termination of specific tasks and the beginning of inquiry in the generalized frame of reference. It is at this point that theory emerges from specific practical work. The teacher's role is that of both "follower" and leader; it could not be otherwise if self-appropriated learning and the joy of discovery are the aim.

With the student's discovery of the "conjectural idea," which in the inquiry model should cohere when the cluster of phenomenal units through analysis yields insight into the critical incident, the practical component of the educational experience may be abandoned. What has been learned through an observed, practical sequence may be articulated in the seminar to illuminate the larger implications, which constitutes the theoretical component. At this stage the teacher's function may assume more traditional proportions: guidance and management in the written or oral presentation of the learning that was accomplished, suggestions, criticism, and the like. At this point, too, the student may assume a conventional role not unlike the one we see in traditional classroom activity. But the heart of the process has been student-centered, and the role of the teacher has been non-authoritative.

Getzels observed that "the human being is not only a stimulus-reducing but a stimulus-seeking organism. He strives not only to master problems with which he is confronted but to confront problems in order to master them."[67] In the seminar-laboratory mode as described, students are given the opportunity to confront and to master—within the definition of "mastery" for the specific pedagogical aim—a problem by means of developing a process. Understanding of principles is achieved through the articulated outcomes of practical experiences. The whole is effected through the triadic elements of teaching, learning, and the vehicle or method in which the teaching-learning process is formulated.

SUMMARY

Asheim has noted that while all library schools continually make curricular changes, "much of this activity is dictated by considerations other than that of providing the most desirable learning experience."[68] Where change has resulted in an increasing emphasis upon the theoretical, this thrust has left little meaningful place in the curriculum for forms of systematic and structured work contacts; the result is a disequilibrium between principles and practice. In the experience of many library educators, this imbalance often engenders disaffection in the student body and, for some faculty, a vague, unarticulated feeling of discontent.

To the several suggestions for work contacts discussed in Chapter 3 may be added the idea of library-centered library education, most ably propounded by Patricia B. Knapp. Her definition of this kind of educational experience included the use of the library as a systematically organized body of resources, with a bibliographic structure that mirrors, however rudely, the structure of the disciplines of recorded knowledge. For Knapp it was self-evident that prospective practitioners of librarianship must gain wide acquaintance with the literature of their field. To that end she posed the not-so-obvious question: What is the literature of librarianship?

Knapp's classification divided into three areas, discrete only for purposes of analysis: 1) the literature related to the practice of librarianship, including the organizational and functional context in which it is practiced; 2) the "body of knowledge" upon which librarianship is based, which has not yet been clearly defined; and 3) the literature librarians deal with, that is, everything.

If mastery means mastery of *content*, then the first category is easiest to define. The literature produced by and for the library profession is not unlike the literature produced by and for other professions and disciplines. It consists of the typical primary and secondary source materials that extend from the most general guides and bibliographies to the esoteric tools of specific subject areas. As the demands of specialization grow, the degree of mastery of content becomes more difficult to determine as a function of formal preparation vis-à-vis on-the-job training. But in this category content can at least be circumscribed.

Librarians and library educators disagree in attempting to construct parameters for a clearly defined body of knowledge upon which librarianship is based. According to Knapp, a few claim that classification theory alone displays the characteristics of a true science; some view the problem as the study of metalanguages or symbology; yet others cite the subject matters of history, sociology, mathematics, psychology, cybernetics, and the like as the proper study of "other disciplines upon which librarianship draws." Clearly, however, such definitions have a way of sliding inevitably into the third category. Epistemologically speaking, librarianship embraces everything; the question of mastery in this context becomes academic.[69]

If a mode of instruction is based on a content-centered concept, with "mastery" as the goal, that method, in Knapp's judgment, is doomed to failure. Instead, Knapp recommended methods that would result in an articulation of structure and the provision of discovery of principles. Such a methodology, she argued, would "help students acquire a conceptual framework" and "a theoretical foundation for a continuing process of learning."[70]

Knapp's initial category included the organizational and functional context in which librarianship is practiced, suggesting that in the process of learning about the literature of librarianship, the principles of organization, control, dissemination and the like be made a concomitant unit of study. The framework thus effected redeems content by making it manageable and reveals those processes by which content is directed to a logical end. Moreover, there should be a balance between the joy of discovery through student-appropriated learning and the structure provided by the teacher which would minimize haphazard and unproductive learning experiences.

But if Knapp's ideas would work using the university library as the center of the learning experiences, might it not work as well using the library science library as a experiential laboratory? In the literature of library science little is found on the possibilities of the library school library as an innovative partner in the educative process; rather the literature deals with library school libraries in terms of facilities, design, and the adequacy of materials for practice and for reading assignments. Several educators proposed that the collection "serve as a model of effective, modern library practice,"[71] by which was meant an operational unit dispensing services and performing research activities. Negatively, a good separate collection would reduce student and faculty use of the parent library, since "library school students are often responsible for the physical destruction of important bibliographic tools through their casual and careless examination of them for meaningless class assignments."[72] There is scant evidence, in short, that the library school library has been proposed as a creative and innovative environment within the instructional context.

Nevertheless, the abject sterility and poverty of traditional modes of instruction oblige us to pursue all methods that might enhance the teaching-learning process while providing a framework in which the theory-practice chestnut can be roasted *and* cracked. Sufficient intellectual justification for a library-centered learning experience utilizing the unit known as the library school collection can be found in the formulations of Knapp, the constructs suggested by Williamson and Reece, and the model provided by Dubin and Taveggia. That is to say, the vehicle for the teaching-learning process in this experience would be a combination of face-to-face instruction and the laboratory component, or in curricular terms, the "seminar-laboratory" course. The former serves as the means by which the teacher makes manifest the student discoveries through the medium of the latter.

A sequence of "seminar-laboratory" instruction would be of little value if the experiential component were not devised to be merely exemplary of the intellectual and theoretical content. To achieve this goal critical incident theory, as applied to educational research, may be assayed. Biddle has suggested conceptual models for accommodating critical incident technique to both the teaching and the learning process. For students a record of "phenomenal units" unexamined at the time of notation would yield to the task of the teacher to examine these data in order to discern "analytic units," patterns of "criticalness," out of a seemingly random sequence of discrete entities.

In theory, the phenomenal units and the analytic units are mutually exclusive. In a sound teaching-learning experience, students ought to become, after trial and error, reasonably adept at apprehending critical incidents in the analytic process. The Deweyan model of inquiry, as it proceeds from problem identification and selection to reasoning, parallels the reductive process by which a multiplicity of phenomenal units translate into a few meaningful analytic patterns. Thus students, with the guidance of the teacher, should be able to apprehend the transition from diversity to unity; and this critical point will serve to signify the end of the practical sequence and the beginning of the exploration of underlying principles.

A dynamic teaching-learning process requires that teaching strategies exhibit a certain synergetic balance and momentum with learning behaviors. Participant observation falls under the rubric of action research, and when designed for the analysis and evaluation of curricular innovation and experimentation, it becomes the principal analytic tool for action research.

Sympathetic identification with individuals or groups being observed, studies show, will not result in distortion if systematic procedures elicit valid categories for the situation to which they apply. In action research this technique is justified on the basis that the experimental situation is the same as or similar to that in which the findings will be applied.[73]

The role of the teacher as participant observer permits concentration on activities that center in the library school library as a result of student-initiated impetus arising from seminar interaction. As students react in ways that reflect the inquiry model, the teacher as sympathetic observer and mentor can assist in delimiting the activity so as to make sense of the phenomenal units, and help the student apprehend critical incident configuration. The unfocused problem, at first perplexing and undefined, is transformed by a process of inquiry into an ordered situation. This in turn may create a new indeterminate situation and give rise to new inquiry. But in every instance, if the model works well, the process has been student-initiated and student-centered, while the role of the teacher has been non-directive, in the Rogerian sense. If the search for a resolution (not necessarily a "solution") to the theory-practice problem is not to be abandoned, library educators must decide if methods like the above, however fraught with risk, are not more deserving than the time-dishonored *ex cathedra* mode of instruction.

REFERENCES

[1]W. Bernard Lukenbill, "Content or Process: A Personal Look at Experiential Learning," *Journal of Education for Librarianship*, 16 (Winter, 1976), 195-96.

[2]R. S. Peters, *Ethics and Education* (Glenview, Illinois: Scott, Foresman and Co., 1967), p. 119.

[3]Patricia B. Knapp, "The Library-Centered Library School," (State University of New York at Albany: Conference on the Bibliographic Control of Library Science Literature, April 19-20, 1968), pp. 1-5. (Mimeographed.)

[4]Ibid., p. 2.

[5]Jerome S. Bruner, *The Process of Education* (New York: Vintage Books, 1961), p. 31.

[6]Knapp, op. cit., p. 4.

[7]Ibid., pp. 4-8.

[8]Ibid., pp. 8-9, 13, 22-23.

[9]Patricia B. Knapp, *The Monteith College Library Experiment* (New York: Scarecrow Press, 1966), pp. 80-84.

[10]Patricia B. Knapp, "The Meaning of the Monteith College Library Program for Library Education," *Journal of Education for Librarianship*, 6 (Fall, 1965), 121-25.

[11]Ibid., pp. 126-27.

[12]*See* the author's article "The Theory-Practice Problem and Library-Centered Library Education," *Journal of Education for Librarianship*, 14 (Fall, 1973), 119-28.

[13]David Kaser, "Library School Libraries," *Journal of Education for Librarianship*, 5 (Summer, 1964), 17.

[14]J. Periam Danton, *Education for Librarianship* (Unesco Public Library Manuals, I) (Paris: Unesco, 1949), pp. 48-53. *See also* Knapp, "The Library-Centered Library School," op. cit., p. 6.

[15]Margaret E. Monroe, "Graduate Library Education in Space," *Journal of Education for Librarianship*, 5 (Summer, 1964), 7-9.

[16]Robert N. Broadus, "Northern Illinois University," *Journal of Education for Librarianship*, 5 (Summer, 1964), 35-36.

[17]Dorothy Bevis, "University of Washington," *Journal of Education for Librarianship*, 5 (Summer, 1964), 47-48.

[18]Kaser, op. cit., p. 19.

[19]Monroe, op. cit., p. 5.

[20]Brian Land, "Library School Quarters and Space—The Ideal," *Journal of Education for Librarianship*, 7 (Fall, 1966), 73-76, 78.

[21]Robert B. Downs, "Quarters and Facilities: An Administrator's Point of View," *Journal of Education for Librarianship*, 7 (Fall, 1966), 86-87.

[22]Irving Lieberman, "Library School Quarters for the Best Educational Practice," *Journal of Education for Librarianship*, 7 (Fall, 1966), 91.

[23]Norman D. Stevens, "The Continuing Conflict," *Journal of Education for Librarianship*, 9 (spring, 1969), 310-11.

[24]Brian Land, "Quarters," *Drexel Library Quarterly*, 3 (January, 1967), 40. And Robert Lee, "The Special Collection in Librarianship," (State University of New York at Albany: Conference on the Bibliographic Control of Library Science Literature, April 19-20, 1968), p. 1 (Mimeographed.)

[25]Madeline Niederhauser, "Professional Collection for Librarians," *Library Occurent*, 23 (February, 1969), 11-12.

[26]Rosamond B. Wetmore, "A Guide to the Organization of Library Collections for the Use of Students of Library Science" (Muncie, Indiana: Ball State University, 1969). (Microfilm.)

[27]N. C. Truax, "Proposed Plan for Furnishing the Department of Library Science Library at the University of Mississippi" (Unpublished master's thesis, University of Mississippi, 1969).

[28]Elspeth Pope and Katherine Armitage, "Status of Library School Librarians," *Journal of Education for Librarianship*, 11 (Spring, 1971), 343.

[29]Ronald L. Fingerson, "The Library Science Library: A Necessary Duplication," *Journal of Education for Librarianship*, 13 (Winter, 1973), 193-97.

[30]Letter, Don L. Lanier, response to Fingerson, *Journal of Education for Librarianship*, 13 (Spring, 1973), 284.

[31]McGrath, op. cit., pp. 290-91.

[32]Williamson, op. cit., p. 61.

[33]Reece, op. cit., p. 121.

[34]Metcalf et al., op. cit., p. 41.

[35]Dewey's instrumental theory of inquiry has been traced from the opening essay of *Studies in Logical Theory* (1903) to the five-step paradigm in *How We Think* (1910, 1933), the chapter "Experience and Thinking" in *Democracy and Education* (1916), the fuller, more sophisticated rendering in *Logic: The Theory of Inquiry* (1938) and elsewhere.

[36]Carl R. Rogers, "Personal Thoughts on Teaching and Learning," *Selected Educational Heresies*, ed. William F. O'Neill (Glenview, Illinois: Scott, Foresman and Co., 1969), p. 210.

[37]Charles Martell, "Age of Creative Insecurity: Student-Centered Learning," *Journal of Education for Librarianship*, 15 (Fall, 1974), 113-14.

[38]Robert S. Morison, *Students and Decision Making*, A Report by [the Author], Chairman of Cornell's Commission on Student Involvement in Decision Making (Washington, D.C.: Public Affairs Press, 1970), p. 42.

[39]Patricia B. Knapp, *The Monteith College Library Experiemnt*, op. cit., p. 40.

[40]Ibid., p. 153.

[41]W. W. Charters and I. B. Whitley, *Analysis of Secretarial Duties and Traits* (Baltimore: Williams and Wilkins, 1924).

[42]John C. Flanagan, "The Critical Incident Technique," *Psychological Bulletin*, 51 (July, 1954), 327-58.

[43]Lewis B. Mayhew, "The Critical Incident Technique in Educational Evaluation," *Journal of Educational Research*, 49 (April, 1956), 591-98.

[44]Carter V. Good, *Introduction to Educational Research* (New York: Appleton-Century-Crofts, 1959), pp. 238-39.

[45]Steven M. Jung, "Evaluative Uses of Unconventional Measurement Techniques in an Educational System," *California Journal of Educational Research*, 22 (March, 1971), 51-52.

[46]John C. Flanagan and Steven M. Jung, "An Illustration: Evaluating a Comprehensive Educational System," *Evaluative Research: Strategies and Methods* (Pittsburgh: American Institute for Research, 1970), pp. 130-46.

[47]Bruce J. Biddle, "Methods and Concepts in Classroom Research," *Review of Educational Research*, 37 (June, 1967), 343.

[48]Mayhew (op. cit., p. 595) cited as a contribution of critical incident technique the establishment of "categories of behaviors for which criteria of success are still largely undefined."

[49]Biddle, op. cit., p. 342.

[50]Mayhew, op. cit., pp. 596, 598.

[51]John Dewey, *Logic: The Theory of Inquiry* (New York: Henry Holt and Co., Inc., 1938), p. 104.

[52]John Dewey, *How We Think* (Boston: D. C. Heath and Co., 1910), p. 78.

[53]Ibid., pp. 72, 76-77.

[54]Michael Polanyi, *Personal Knowledge* (Chicago: University of Chicago Press, 1958), passim.

[55]Douglas Waples and Ralph W. Tyler, *Research Methods and Teachers' Problems* (New York: McMillan, 1930), p. 12.

[56]Frederick L. Whitney, *The Elements of Research* (New York: Prentice-Hall, 1946), p. 168.

[57]Waples and Tyler, op. cit., pp. vii-ix, quoting John Dewey, *Sources of a Science of Education* (New York: Horace Liveright, 1929). Of this monograph, the authors remarked that it "gives much needed emphasis to the fact that only as all sources are examined for evidence bearing directly on the actual business of teaching are we developing a genuine science of education. The notion that laboratory studies in contributory sciences, such as educational psychology, constitute contributions to educational science whether they ever affect the work of the classroom or not, is sufficiently widespread to deserve emphatic repudiation."

[58]Hollis L. Caswell, "Foreword," in Stephen M. Corey, *Action Research to Improve School Practices* (New York: Teachers College, Columbia University, 1953), pp. v-vi.

[59]Stephen M. Corey, *Action Research to Improve School Practices* (New York: Teachers College, Columbia University, 1953), p. 6.

[60]Good, op. cit., p. 241.

[61]George J. Mouly, *The Science of Educational Research*, 2nd ed. (New York: Van Nostrand, 1970), p. 287.

[62]Abraham Shumsky, *The Action Research Way of Learning* (New York: Teachers College, Columbia University, 1958), p. 202.

[63]Mouly, op. cit., p. 288n.

[64]Morris S. Schwartz and Charlotte G. Schwartz, "Problems in Participant Observation," *American Journal of Sociology*, 60 (January, 1955), 350.

[65]Good, op. cit., p. 227.

[66]Ibid., p. 241.

[67]J. W. Getzels, "Creative Thinking, Problem Solving, and Instruction," *Theories of Learning and Instruction*, The Sixty-third Yearbook of the National Society for the Study of Education, Part I, ed. Ernest R. Hilgard (Chicago: University of Chicago Press, 1964), p. 266.

[68]Lester Asheim, "New Trends in the Curriculum of Library Schools," *Education for Librarianship: The Design of the Curriculum of Library Schools* (Papers Presented at a Conference on the Design of the Curriculum of Library Schools Conducted by the University of Illinois Graduate School of Library Science, September 6-9, 1970), ed. Herbert Goldhor (Urbana, Illinois: University of Illinois Graduate School of Library Science, 1971), p. 65.

[69]Knapp, "The Library-Centered Library School," op. cit., pp. 6-8.

[70]Ibid., pp. 9, 22-23.

[71]Lee, op. cit., p. 3; Land, "Quarters," p. 40; Monroe, p. 8; Downs, p. 87.

[72]Stevens, loc. cit.

[73]Arthur W. Foshay and James A. Hall, *Research in Curriculum Improvement* (Washington: Association for Supervision and Curriculum Development, 1957 Yearbook, 1957), pp. 43-44.

5

TOWARD A RESOLUTION OF
THEORY AND PRACTICE

INTRODUCTION

During the 1970s, discourse on the theory-practice problem was addressed in the literature obliquely rather than directly, a departure from the vigorous, sometimes acrimonious, arguments of earlier decades. This relative absence of concern appears to have coincided with the energy and anguish library educators have invested in the debate about "information science" and its appropriate place in the curricula of graduate library schools. Schools of library science, fearing opprobrium from some vaguely defined Authority, hastened to add the holy words to the name of their institutions. At least one school, Syracuse, expunged the offensive word "library" from its name, as if no such social agency existed that was worthy of study. All of this effort is ironic when one considers the statement by one of the most vociferous of information science cheerleaders: "The problems with foundations for information science education are obvious in the fact that we have to deal with a diversity of theories, that we lack a basic theory; we don't as yet have our basic principles. . . . We have a great deal of knowledge, but it is fragmented knowledge."[1]

Modes of instruction in library education seem to have suffered a relative diminution of interest; one cannot be sure whether this too is related to the information science angst. A study, published in 1978, asked respondents to indicate the "probability" and "desirability" of twenty events that might occur in the future and which might influence libraries and library education. One of the projected "events" in this Delphi-technique questionnaire was phrased as follows:

The "classical" lecture method ended in 40 percent of library schools by teaching machines, closed circuit TV, interactive TV, audio-visual aids, and computer-assisted instruction.

The response to this occurrence was interesting; it did *not* seem "probable" to the majority of the participants and "it was regarded as 'almost' neutral on its desirability or undesirability."[2] So much for the degree of concern about the innovative possibilities of technology as a means of enhancing teaching and learning, the very technology that comprises the artifacts of "information science."

Where the literature of the 1970s does reveal an interest in the practical component of library education, the articles largely extol the virtues of field experience, whether that is called a practicum, an internship, a traineeship, or simply field work. One study, a part of a doctoral dissertation, summarized the feelings of library educators about student work contacts prior to graduation. Those respondents who favored omitting or limiting field work cited as reasons: "administrative difficulties (size of student body, relative inadequacy in number and quality of available libraries with librarians willing to cooperate, the lack of library school control over the experience, inadequate supervision on the part of the cooperating library's staff); unnecessary, since students get library experience on their own; low priority compared to course work; ineffective in relation to other activities; narrowing; burdensome on libraries and their patrons; undue emphasis on clerical activities; trend away from field work in library education."

Positive response to field experiences concurrent with classroom instruction included: "students and employers favor it; theory and practice can be related; students are oriented to reality; learning is applied; certification procedures require it; field work compensates for professional positions which provide no supervision or orientation to the field; student confidence is built; competence, judgment are developed; course work is enhanced (student gets more, given more); student's program of study is individualized; acquaintance is made with patrons; faculty are updated; special courses are extended."[3]   That most of these reasons could have been cited in any of the last decades since Williamson gives one an indolent feeling of déjà vu and seems to demonstrate that the pros and cons of field work will wax and wane forever without essentially changing.

Proponents of a strong information science element in library education inveigh against what they perceive as an outdated curriculum. An appropriate course for the "almost totally information-dependent post-industrial era" must of necessity "seek to study and analyze objectively the fundamental components and links within the total information transfer chain." This curriculum would   "lead to a more pervasive and in-depth study and analysis of the principles of librarianship—principles applicable for the management of recorded information in traditional as well as non-traditional information service environments. . . . Curricula based *not* so much on pragmatic as on theoretical considerations."[4]

Theoreticians of information studies usually write pugnaciously; they often see "librarianship" as the enemy. Often, too, they construct simplistic dichotomies and attempt to demolish them as would a dunce who destroys gnats with a mallet. Yet not one argument in the entire corpus of putative "information science" literature can be found to gainsay the need for a practical component in the brave new curriculum. On the contrary, the "new professional," armed with slide rule and computer print-out, is perhaps in need of *more* of a dose of the practical in his library education than is his benighted traditional counterpart. Or, as one apologist for the new curriculum affirmed, "a professional persons should be capable of being a *practitioner* within a given system, a *designer* of such a system or of a subsystem within that system, an *evaluator* of the system or sub-system, an *administrator* of the system or sub-system, and, finally an *in-service trainer* within the system or sub-system." But the curriculum that produces this exemplar of virtuosity must allow the "appropriate periods of practical experience preceding and intervening between the various stages."[5]

The rational mind will not permit the information scientist (those who insist upon the logical contiguity of "information" and "science" have little understanding of themselves or of the world) to promulgate a false dualism: information science *versus* library science. The insights and technologies that comprise information studies are as amenable to the resolution of theory and practice as the traditional elements of the curriculum. What follows is an attempt to place information studies in the larger perspective of education for librarianship as that education relates to the theory-practice problem in the teaching-learning process.

THE INFORMATION COMPONENT IN THE THEORY-PRACTICE EQUATION

Permit me to adopt Shera's excellent definition, a distinction that in my judgement establishes a condign relationship between librarianship and information studies.

> Librarianship is the generic term and information science is an area of research which draws its substance, methods, and techniques from a variety of disciplines to achieve an understanding of the properties, behavior, and flow of information. Information science is not souped-up librarianship or information retrieval, nor is it antithetical to either. Rather information science contributes to the theoretical and intellectual base for the librarian's operations.[6]

Accordingly, to the extent that teaching about and research on the information transfer process enriches the curriculum, the need to find the proper balance of theory and experience in this area seems manifest. We exclude the information studies component of the curriculum from the theory-practice mix at our peril. As Buckland noted in a discerning discussion of the issue, "A continuing problem in library school administration is achieving the proper interaction of theory and practice. . . . Theory of any kind is necessarily a sterile activity unless at some point it is related to and tested against reality. . . . It follows from this that information science must do more than be a theoretical activity. It must relate in some way to *activity* involving access to information."   Nor can there be an isolation of the faculty who teach information studies within a library school: "Information scientists who are in a separate department run a serious risk of jeopardizing their own long-term progress as well as reducing the chances of contributing to the progress of others . . . if we define information science as primarily a theoretical activity, we should expect negligible prospects for information scientists."   What is needed, Buckland averred, is "an integrating drive to redress the damage done by the tendency to separate information science from librarianship." Moreover, when so-called "information scientists" attempt to impose their jargon and pseudointellectual constructs upon students in a library school without an appropriate understanding of the basic tenets of librarianship, they are justly open to the wry definition "of information science as librarianship taught by amateurs."[7]

If our analysis of the theory-practice issue in the preceding chapters is sound, one may reasonably infer that the modes of instruction and the philosophy of inquiry will serve to effect a reconciliation of theory and practice within the framework of information studies as it will for library studies. The arguments for a substantial theoretical base need no belaboring; they are grounded a priori in the mission of the professional school within the university. As Swanson notes, "With respect to a balance between theory and practice, it seems to me possible and perhaps even desirable that some courses be almost exclusively devoted to theory and some to practice."[8] An alternative to that division was proposed by Osborn in 1970. To the extent that computer technology pervades library operations, "work should be redistributed throughout the curriculum so that computer topics fit in naturally whenever and wherever they belong."[9] But whether information studies should be taught as discrete units of "theory" or "practice" or whether the total curriculum should be infused with the concepts of information in its societal implications, the requirements of both a theoretical and a practical constituent are apposite. "People who learn from a principles point of view," Swanson points out,   "who really understand principles and concepts, seem best able to cope with problems in a real life situation. They are able to use principles to build a problem-solving strategy or procedure for the newly encountered problem, if this is the way their learning has been acquired. In a given course, we can't ever teach about all of the situations that can arise; we can only provide illustrations to facilitate learning principles and how they can be used."[10] In these comments we observe echoes of Dewey and McGrath: the inquiring mind and the need to provide only enough illustrations to illuminate the theory upon which practice is based.

If the "seminar-laboratory" mode of instruction is a viable construct for the resolution of theory and practice, then, in principle, it ought to be able to accommodate that congeries of products and services for the information component. No one library school library can hope to reflect in its holdings and operations all exemplary conditions that will be encountered by the novitiate in his professional career. But those schools that have accepted the value of a separate collection harnassed to the instructional program will endeavor to provide the materials for information studies. The unit that we have been calling a "library school library" can be fluidly defined to include developments in mediagraphy, computational hardware, microform technology, and the like. Indeed, it will be necessary to do this if education for librarianship is ever going to rise to meet and, ideally, anticipate advances in information theory and technology. To the extent that library schools can afford to expand existing library *and* information resources to reflect the new, the library science library qua laboratory becomes a more faithful vehicle for pre-professional practice and its concurrent reconciliation in theory.

New information environments are grafted upon existing structures; rarely do they spring full blown from the brow of the architect or engineer. Where a library science library can accommodate by addition or absorption audiovisual equipment, microforms, computer terminals, and related forms of automation, opportunities for students to explore the theoretical bases of these practical tools are enhanced. The crucial pedagogical issue concerns the manner in which alternatives to the traditional, book-oriented systems are effected in the curriculum. In a library-centered, practice-theory sequence, relationships must emerge organically, must arise from responses to inquiry in problem-solving activities. Simply to graft the new technologies onto exercises of this kind would be to create a learning situation that is artificial, turgid, and pretentious.

Reflection upon the egregious enthusiasms that some library educators have displayed toward the tools that have become equated with "information science" suggests a warning. As Asheim pointed out, "The impact of the new technology seems to have been primarily that of creating new how-to-do-it courses for old ones." Moreover, "the typing of hundreds of catalog cards, the running down of prepared questions to illustrate the features of reference tools — these pedagogical exercises are being laughed out of existence. But in their place we have students sitting for hours before consoles typing out predetermined code numbers, and searching for answers to prepared questions through MARC tapes instead of the books themselves. The method would appear to be as rote as ever. . . . Checking something in the card catalog is still checking something in the card catalog, even if we do now call it 'querying a store.' "[11]

I have no objection to renaming the locus of this activity the "library and information science library" or even the "information laboratory," if that will mollify the attenuated sensibilities of my "information science" colleagues. But there is a real danger in the trivialization of the practical component of information studies. The nature of new processes is such that once the professional challenge is over, they are (quite properly) relegated to the status of routines. But to the student, the initial encounter is a discovery, and he must be given the chance to gain at least a cursory familiarity. In the seminar-laboratory mode described in the preceding chapter, the conditions permitting trivialized learning cannot occur; for the theory-practice model insists that the McGrath criterion be scrupulously followed. As in the traditional inquiry areas, the theoretical emphasis is not sacrificed to the practical regardless of the initial fascination with the technological toy which tempts the student into practice excesses. In discussing some conceptual problems of a learning laboratory for library education, Harm noted that students "will learn to operate [the new equipment] in order to make full use of the laboratory," but the tools "will not be an end in themselves. The biology student must learn to operate a microscope in order to function in the lab but the pitfall to avoid is that of confusing microscopes with biology."[12]

The "true potential of the profession of librarianship," according to Taylor, resides in learned skills which can be brought to bear both within and outside the library marketplace, in   "the ability to organize information; knowledge of the variety, range, and usefulness of information resources; a commitment to service, i.e., a sensitivity to needs and uses of information and a desire to match those needs."   Taylor, Dean of the Syracuse School of Information Studies (who, interestingly, rejects the phrase "information science" because it is appropriate "only for such concerns as general systems theory, cybernetics, artificial intelligence, etc."), reported that "about 25 percent of the Syracuse graduates are going into nonlibrary but information-related positions."[13] But another quoted statistic puts the number of librarians who do work in traditional settings as high as 99 percent.[14] While it is probably futile to play the numbers game, it may be posited that at least a majority of library school graduates will be working in some kind of entity known as a library (or a library and information center, if you will) for the foreseeable future.

As I noted in the preceding chapter, Knapp's idea of library-centered library education rests on the fundamental assumption that graduates of schools of library and/or information science will be working in libraries. We need no more apologize for her assumption than we need to ask Jesse Shera to defend the title of his magnum opus *The Foundations of Education for Librarianship*. It has been argued in the foregoing chapters that the skills to be learned through the instrumentality of the seminar-laboratory are disciplined inquiry, attention to phenomenal detail, ability to generalize from critical configurations, and capacity to grasp theoretical concepts with minimal emphasis on those routine tasks that illuminate the theory.

It is difficult to say (and in any event beyond the scope of this study) if the teaching-learning processes set forth for library-centered library education will provide the tools of disciplined analysis and observation to equip the student for every non-library position in the burgeoning information industry. If, in Taylor's words, the "office of the future will become an electronic library," perhaps the library of the future will simply be known as an "information center." Indeed, many librarians and library educators join the work *library* to the phrase *information center* when they lecture or contribute to the literature. I am persuaded that, whatever future transmutations take place institutionally, there will exist a structure in which recorded knowledge is stored and processed. Almost all organized entities, Taylor believes, are "basically specialized systems concerned with acquiring, organizing, and disseminating information, and provide information, referral, and counseling service to clients. All of these systems and services have need for the skills which presumably library schools develop in their students. When these skills are seen in a context in which the library is but one of the beneficiaries, their true value becomes apparent."[15]

But while we await Taylor's millennium, we must resolve the problem of the relationship of theory and experience within the framework of both library and information studies; and this can be accomplished by means of the models suggested in this monograph. To elevate information science technology to some fatuous metaphysics is to derogate its legitimate authority and value and to invite the trenchant definition of information science as comprising "those topics taught in library schools that were not in the curriculum of the Graduate Library School in Chicago in 1950."[16]

SUGGESTIONS, REFLECTIONS, CONCLUSIONS

In developing a set of principles to resolve the problem of theory and practice in library education, "we tread upon a superficially familiar but highly unknown terrain which is wide open to exploration, with a multitude of theoretical approaches which can be taken."[17] Moreover, the difficulties of prosecuting any sort of curricular innovation are intimidating. Heiss's extensive survey of graduate schools proclaimed the melancholy fact that most faculty members loathe curriculum planning on a departmental or campus-wide basis and "in general have little aptitude for it."[18]

Even in instances where cooperation and enthusiasm for experimentation are assured, devising a conceptual structure for a specific need may yield results favorable only to the situation at hand. The achievement of internal goals is almost always difficult to replicate, and this seems especially true when the experiment emphasizes individual learning behaviors and perforce entails a sacrifice of elegant design to a fidelity that more nearly mirrors the groping, awkward nature of intellectual striving. The pattern of research in the teaching-learning process over the decades suggests the difficulty of developing a unifying theory. As Biddle noted, "although a wide variety of classroom phenomena has in fact been investigated, it is difficult for both the reviewer and the investigators to understand the relationship between their findings and those of others."[19] That is to say, the very fecundity of approaches hinders the development of an inclusive, empirically based theory of instruction.

Numerous attempts have been made to individualize instruction, based upon the "extremely plausible" argument that "learners do differ in ways relevant to their ability to profit from different kinds of instruction, content, incentives, and the like. Almost by definition, instruction adapted to these individual differences should be more effective." The authors of the above statement, Gage and Unruh, then proceed to puzzle over the failure of researchers to find dramatic results for forms of individualized instruction. "Why," they ask, "are not the mean scores on achievement measures of pupils taught with due respect for their individual needs and abilities substantially higher, in unmistakable ways, than those of students taught in the conventional classroom, where everybody reads the same book, listens to the same lecture, participates in the same classroom discussion, moves at the same pace, and works at the same problems? For the fact is that, despite several decades of concern with individualization few if any striking results have been reported."[20]

The authors then suggest what common sense tells us: the "conventional" classroom does not necessarily produce conventional learning. Students individualize instruction for themselves: "Perhaps the time is ripe for a re-examination of assumptions about what goes on in the conventional classroom." On the other hand, they note that improved methods of individualization may make a major difference in outcomes. To pursue both areas is the task of future researchers, but Gage and Unruh are not sanguine that a methodological breakthrough will be readily or easily achieved.[21]

Despite the fact that we probably know little more about the mysteries of the teaching-learning process than did Plato, we cannot avoid rushing in where neither fools nor angels tread. The emphasis in library-centered library education (which combines the features of the "conventional" classroom with the experimental situation) is upon the analogy of the library school library as an educational laboratory, for it is essential to our conceptual framework that the learning environment be that of a working library, with not only all the current tools of information technology but also the imperfections that are shared in varying degree with other operational units. In such a learning environment, exceptions must be made, compromise with total reality must be effected, simulation must be introduced. The guiding principle in compromising reality must be the efficacy of educational aims generally and an emphasis on the theoretical component specifically. Within that very broad framework a variety of teaching-learning strategies may be assayed.

But there are arguments for the idea of the library as *being* a laboratory, where conditions—though simulated—could be so arranged that a number of permutations and combinations of diverse realities would be presented for exploration. The educational advantages in this model are as obvious as the limitations. Modular elements could emphasize now this aspect of librarianship, now that one. Students would not have to wait upon "what is" to pursue deliberately and artificially created events. Lost, however, would be the "feel" of a library known to be grounded in reality and functioning in an actual as well as a pedagogical situation. In the model of the library *as* laboratory, response to problematic events would more nearly resemble "practice" work, albeit on a sophisticated level. The creation of a fully-equipped "collapsible" laboratory to simulate a variety of hypothetical library problems would involve a large investment of time and funds. But there is no question that experimental control could be greatly strengthened.

If increased options for practical work through simulation or with the new technologies do not automatically confer upon the teaching-learning process a greater quality, neither does adherence to a proven set of teaching measures appreciably demonstrate a significant difference in instructional outcomes. We are not at all sure about our ability to prove statistically the main effects of any currently used educational or instructional variable. One methodological alternative that may be apposite to our situation concerns identifying the "problem-solving" student. Getzels noted that current trends in education have called "for instructional methods (and materials) emphasizing the ability to see generalizations in specifics, to discover, to ask fruitful questions." To foster this quality in classroom learning, emphasis must be placed upon "discovered problems" rather than "presented problems" and attention must be directed to latent cognitive processes that will reveal "divergent" as well as "convergent" thinking. The process that stresses presented problems is typical of traditional instruction, in which "the problem is given (is known) and there is a standard method for solving it, known to the problem-solver (student, experimental subject) and to others (teacher, experimenter) and guaranteeing a solution." In the experimental, non-traditional setting, "the problem itself exists but remains to be identified or discovered, and no standard method for solving it is known to the problem-solver or to the others."[22] The latter, which has been called the "dynamic-heuristic"[23] model, is most desirable in library-centered library education in which theoretical insights arise from the solving of practical problems through the inquiry process.

Unfortunately, there are difficulties suggested by the establishment of identification criteria for the potentially creative problem-solving student. The kind of internship Stallmann proposed (see Chapter 2) was an elite model. When the "best" students are recruited into a program which is competitive and limited in number, it is difficult to validate the method. The students are likely to succeed by virtue of ability in any event. Moreover, they are likely to absorb problem-solving skills for use in their professional careers whatever the curriculum offered. The Williamson criterion – the selection of students who have not shown proficiency in their ability "to see generalizations in specifics" in traditional courses – would be ignored. Indeed, Williamson argued for a model the opposite of the gifted problem-solver. In his remarks on "the fundamental purpose of field experience," he stated:

> If the purpose is to acquire skill, then future work and present interests should be the determining factor. If grasp of principles and better understanding of subjects taught is the purpose, then the practical work, if it cannot cover all subjects, should be selected to represent the branches in which the student *has not shown proficiency* (emphasis added).[24]

Another difficulty involves the manner of selection itself. Should library schools require of entering students yet another standardized or ad hoc examination that purports to predict abilities in divergent thinking and problem-solving? Or would it not be more rewarding to take the less-gifted student into a program in which there is difficulty enough assessing what the relevant variables are for clinching theory and practice?

Evaluative options in library-centered library education must transcend the multiple-choice test or the essay examination if they are to be meaningful. Two kinds of evaluation seem particularly suited: that involving individual assessment, which permits non-traditional reporting; and that in which the efforts of the group are judged and by inference acknowledge the precise contribution of the individual. Concerning the former, options other than the traditional research paper should be sought and tried; their viability as evaluative instruments must not be prejudiced in advance. The latter assessment is more difficult, for it reflects an anomaly in our very conduct of schooling. As Bruner noted, "we require of our students that they compete with each other in their studies yet urge upon them the utmost cooperativeness in other forms of activity."[25] And librarianship is nothing if not an enterprise in social cooperation in the service of intellectual ends.

If curricular experimentation were to demonstrate that average students are capable of apprehending the relationship between theory and practice through library-centered library education at least as well as by traditional, deferred methods, what criteria need be applied to determine its validation in professional practice? That is, may one approach this kind of assessment with confidence when the non-experimental populations in professional groups have not shown an expected relation between ability in school and professional competence?

The results of longitudinal studies where they have been conducted are discouraging indeed. Two studies of physicians which purported to measure "the quality of professional competence" found no significant relationship between subsequent achievement based on a number of critical variables, including "theoretical contributions" to the science of medicine, and the medical school from which the physician graduated, his college admission test score, his class rank, or the length of his graduate training.[26] In view of the amount of time, effort and money invested in medical education, the results of these studies engendered a not unexpected degree of dismay among medical educators. But Wasserman found the same absence of correlation in the library profession. Assuming as self-evident that "there is some relationship between the grades that students receive for their work and the success of faculty members in teaching whatever it is they try to teach," he discovered not only "that such correlations do not exist" but that "even the reverse may be true."[27]

It would be possible to amass quantifiable data in a follow-up study by citing the graduates' contributions to the scholarly literature, advanced degrees subsequently earned, innovations of an obviously superior nature on-the-job — the visible lineaments of achievement wherein principles were applied to situations that demonstrated a consistent ability in disciplined inquiry. But the results of any follow-up would have to be interpreted with a great deal of care; the art of extrapolation is an elusive and frustrating enterprise. And before any criteria for measuring achievement with the desired degree of specificity can be established, an appropriate time to allow for the opportunity to judge fairly the practitioners' contribution to the manipulation of theory and practice must be designated. Shall a follow-up study be initiated after the student has been in professional work two years, five years, ten years?

Freedom, Relevance, and Discovery

Wasserman has pointed out that "one contemporary doctrine, deeply ingrained in the new young culture of relevance and activism, is that an important ingredient of education is understanding achieved by actually doing or observing or participating." But faculty place little value on experiential forms of learning: "Only uncommonly do professors conceive of themselves as being in the business of helping to extend a student's experience or perception through real observations into genuine areas. . . . Individual experience must be related to professional knowledge and skill . . . in the final analysis librarianship is the practice of one human being reacting upon another. . . . Unless the student is encouraged to translate his method of performance beyond the level of papers and examinations into such a philosophy of commitment, it is all useless."[28]

But in the same article Wasserman also said that "many would argue that without theory or philosophy practice is ultimately ritualistic or bankrupt."[29] In a seminar-laboratory mode students are given the opportunity to measure a specific cluster of institutional tasks against the larger canvas of library principles illuminated in the classroom sessions and aided by the implications of inquiry developed in a research paper or other form of evaluative exercise.

Pluralistic aspects of teaching and learning appear to be pertinent to our discussion of these modes of experiential activities. As Flood posed the question:

> Do we really believe that students are not motivated to become librarians? It would seem so in our tendency to proscribe curricula with little free choice for students. In syllabus development we have a tendency to specify the objectives for the student and make assignments which we think will lead to the attainment of these objectives. What would happen if we were to take the tack that each student would specify what the relevant learnings are for him and what his best route was for attaining them?[30]

If in responding to Flood's question a library school were to permit students the freedom to specify and design their relevant learning situations, would the result be beneficial or anarchic? Put another way, could Osborn's statement, that "if we are to make our curriculum effective, we must do everything within our power to remove the structure from the individual courses,"[31] be reconciled with "the proliferation of a number of unrelated and unrelatable rationales and techniques"[32] that might arise out of the exercise of student freedom in curricular design?

It would appear that freedom and relevance as educational desiderata can be exercised with responsibility if individual projects are prosecuted within a conceptual framework where others may share in the learning process while at the same time pursuing their own defined goals. Not the absence of structure but the provision of a frame of reference encompassing individual needs is requisite, for it is patently impossible under existing conditions to offer a one-to-one relationship in the teaching-learning process.

But even if possible, would a tutorial arrangement be therefore desirable? The profession of librarianship is a series of activities conjointly effected in social intercourse; its operations and services are related one to another in a way which suggests that their formal study should mirror the reality of these relationships. What may be objected to is not structure itself but the structure of discrete, fragmented courses, in which the needs and demands of individual faculty bear often an adventitious relationship to the whole. The argument is the ancient one of diversity in unity, for surely library educators do not wish to impress their preconceived will upon students.

What structure, or conceptual framework, could thus be provided in order to insure responsible student involvement and yet tend toward a unity that is not inimical to self-appropriated learning, that does not merely transmit the status quo, and that does not involve, *ex cathedra*, an authoritarian teaching model? Knapp cogently suggested that such a framework be that of library-centered library education, that the logical structure of the curriculum should include the organization and activities of a library itself. She was persuaded that *res ipsa loquitur*, that the rationale was so obvious it was unassailable. In her analysis of the implications of this model, she acknowledged many problems of style, method and content, but that it was valid conceptually she had no doubt.

Library education in a university milieu assumes that the dominant emphasis in the curriculum consist of a presentation of those constructs, concepts and principles that contribute to verified knowledge, a body of theory. Yet "every profession is a blending of theory and practice, a science and an art, *wissen und können*, to understand and to know how. Both of these elements are essential, both must be maintained in an harmonious and proper relationship. . . . If there is an excess of know-how the profession degenerates into a mere craft, while too much theory leads to the sterility of empty formalism."[33]   That this harmony has not always been achieved in professional education generally and in library education specifically form the burden of argument in Chapters 1 and 2 of this study.

Swank suggested that our teaching of the theory of librarianship has "not been as successful as we would like because . . . we still insist on teaching the theory as though its only utility were to illuminate the practice."[34] Thus one outcome of an experiential component in the curriculum may involve the performance of tasks in which principles are shown to be sound or unsound. Probably the majority of library educators agree that the ideal internship or other work-contact is one in which the student, cognizant of the body of theory he has been given, applies such principles as the tasks reveal. The theory is "utilized" to enhance the quality of practice and the sequence of instruction is vindicated. Whether the practice is concurrent or deferred, the order of identification of principles followed by their application in practice is sacred in most curricula.

This accepted order of things reveals, however, some disconcerting problems. A common complaint in all professional education is that theory separated from practice in time or geographically is often forgotten if indeed it was fully apprehended when presented. Practice offered concurrent with the presentation of theory reduces the difficulties of deferment; a further improvement in balance is achieved when the school controls and manages the practical constituent. But the utilitarian aspect of the theory still dominates this approach, and the student retains, or is strengthened in, the notion that a body of theory exists for the sake of effective practice only. There is the tendency in this order of things to question the principles that have been transmitted little if at all.

Another problem is suggested by Knapp's findings in the Monteith College Library experiment. Where general principles "which underlie the structure of librarianship" are transmitted to students before they seek their validation in practice, the pleasure and power of discovery is absent.[35] If heuristic learning is acknowledged as a pedagogical good, the sequence we have been discussing tends to vitiate the discovery process. Again, utility is achieved at the expense of another value which may be of greater significance in the learning process.

To provide direction within a structure that would not suffocate individual desires and to offer a program that would afford an opportunity to discover the theoretical implications of practical tasks in librarianship and information studies requires creative, time-consuming synergetic activity among faculty, students, and support staff of the library school library, if that is to be the locus of inquiry. Structured direction would accommodate the diversity of learning needs without abandoning learning outcomes to serendipity. Heuristic learning would free the pursuit of principles from its traditional utilitarian habitat in practice. The conceptual framework would, ideally, enhance the discovery of principles in a library-centered environment thus illuminating the relationship between theory and practice in a manner hitherto untried in traditional modes of instruction.

Freedom, relevance, discovery—this triad of interrelated goals requires the somewhat elaborate enabling methodology developed in our analysis of the problem of reconciling theory and practice in the teaching-learning process. The expatiation of these ideas themselves will be perceived by the careful reader as theory, and it is axiomatic that "a theory is not a theory unless it can be disproved," that is, unless "it can be falsified by some possible experimental outcome."[36] If library educators are not to evade pedagogical theory of this kind because it is too enervating or because it is easier to engage in mellifluous discourse upon the gewgaws of technology, it is incumbent upon them to develop multiple working hypotheses to challenge and indeed disprove the assumptions of this study. Whatever alternative strategies emerge as a "theory of practice-theory resolution," the notion that this vexing problem is an irreconcilable dualism should be laid to rest. Like those dualisms that John Dewey called "an isolation of mind from activity,"[37] to characterize theory and practice in antithetical terms serves no useful function in the education for the profession of librarianship.

REFERENCES

[1]Tefko Saracevic, "A Model of Knowledge Communication as a Unifying Framework for Education in Librarianship and Information Science," *Information Reports and Bibliographies*, 7 (1978), 28 (Reprint of the Proceedings of a Conference on Education for Information Science—Strategies for Change in Library School Programs, April 24-25, 1977), ed. Irving M. Klempner.

[2]Martha Boaz, "The Future of Library and Information Science Education," *Journal of Education for Librarianship*, 18 (spring, 1978), 319, 320.

[3]Virginia Witucke, "Library School Policies Toward Preprofessional Work Experience," *Journal of Education for Librarianship*, 16 (Winter, 1976), 166. Taken from the author's "The Place of Library Experience in Library Education" (unpublished D.L.S. dissertation, Columbia University, 1974).

[4]Irving M. Klempner, "The New Imperatives: Decisions for Library School Curricula," *Special Libraries*, 67 (September, 1976), 413-14.

[5]Pauline Wilson, "Impending Change in Library Education: Implications for Planning," *Journal of Education for Librarianship*, 18 (Winter, 1978), 164.

[6]Jesse H. Shera, *The Foundations of Education for Librarianship* (New York: John Wiley and Sons, Inc., 1972), p. 293.

[7]Michael K. Buckland, "Looking Ahead—And Around," *Information Reports and Bibliographies*, op. cit., pp. 16-17.

[8]Rowena W. Swanson, [Comments], *Information Reports and Bibliographies*, op. cit., p. 52.

[9]Andrew D. Osborn, "The Design of the Curriculum for the Third Era of Education for Librarianship," *Education for Librarianship: The Design of the Curriculum of Library Schools* (Papers Presented at a Conference on the Design of the Curriculum of Library Schools Conducted by the University of Illinois Graduate School of Library Science, September 6-9, 1970), ed. Herbert Goldhor (Urbana, Illinois: University of Illinois Graduate School of Library Science, 1971), p. 184.

[10.]Swanson, op. cit.

[11]Lester Asheim, "New Trends in the Curriculum of Library Schools," *Education for Librarianship: The Design of the Curriculum of Library Schools*, op. cit., p. 72.

[12]Marvin P. Harm, "Changing from the Traditional Library to a Learning Laboratory" (Paper Presented at the Institute on the Role of the Library School Library, Emory University, May 4, 1971), p. 14. (Mimeographed.)

[13]Robert S. Taylor, "Educational Breakaway," *American Libraries*, 10 (June, 1979), 366, 368.

[14]Klempner, op. cit., p. 411.

[15]Taylor, op. cit., p. 366.

[16]Buckland, op. cit., p. 15.

[17]Neal Harlow, "Designs on the Curriculum," *Education for Librarianship: The Design of the Curriculum of Library Schools*, op. cit., p. 13.

[18]Ann M. Heiss, *Challenges to Graduate Schools* (San Francisco: Josey-Bass, 1970), p. 250.

[19]Bruce J. Biddle, "Methods and Concepts in Classroom Research," *Review of Educational Research*, 37 (June, 1967), 354.

[20]N. L. Gage and W. R. Unruh, "Theoretical Formulations for Research on Teaching," *Review of Educational Research*, 37 (June, 1967), 368.

[21]Ibid., pp. 368-69.

[22]J. W. Getzels, "Creative Thinking, Problem Solving, and Instruction," *Theories of Learning and Instruction*, The Sixty-Third Yearbook of the National Society for the Study of Education, Part I, ed. Ernest R. Hilgard (Chicago: University of Chicago Press, 1964), pp. 241, 257, 265. Getzel's use of "convergent" and "divergent" corresponds to linear and non-linear processes that I envision taking place in the seminar-laboratory inquiry paradigm.

[23]Fred N. Kerlinger, *Foundations of Behavioral Research* (New York: Holt, Rinehart and Winston, 1965), p. 10.

[24]Williamson, op. cit., p. 58.

[25]Jerome S. Bruner, "On the Continuity of Learning," *Saturday Review of Education*, 1 (February 10, 1973), 24.

[26]Philip B. Price et al., "Measurement of Physician Performance," *Journal of Medical Education*, 39 (1964), 203-10; O. L. Peterson et al., "Appraisal of Medical Students' Abilities As Related to Training and Careers after Graduation," *New England Journal of Medicine*, 269 (1963), 1174-82.

[27]Paul Wasserman, "Professional Adaptation: Library Education Mandate," *Library Journal*, 95 (April 1, 1970), 1282.

28Ibid., p. 1286.

29Ibid., p. 1282.

30Barbara Flood, "Some Thoughts on Graduate Education in Librarianship," *Journal of Education for Librarianship*, 12 (Fall, 1971), 133.

31Osborn, op. cit., p. 190.

32James W. Ramey, "General Principles of Curriculum Construction," *Education for Librarianship: The Design of the Curriculum of Library Schools*, op. cit., pp. 84-85.

33Shera, op. cit., pp. 201-202.

34Raynard C. Swank, "Sixth-Year Curricula and the Education of Library School Faculties," *Journal of Education for Librarianship*, 8 (Summer, 1967), 15.

35Patricia B. Knapp, "The Meaning of the Monteith College Library Program for Library Education," *Journal of Education for Librarianship*, 6 (Fall, 1965), 127.

36John R. Platt, "Strong Inference," *Science*, 146 (October 16, 1964), 350.

37John Dewey, *Democracy and Education* (New York: The Free Press, 1966), p. 323.

SELECTED BIBLIOGRAPHY

MONOGRAPHS

Berelson, Bernard. *Graduate Education in the United States.* New York: McGraw-Hill, 1960.

Blauch, Lloyd E., ed. *Education for the Professions.* Washington: GPO, 1971.

Boehm, Werner W., director. *Social Work Curriculum Study.* 14 vols. New York: Council on Social Work Education, 1959.

Bruner, Jerome S. *The Process of Education.* New York: Vintage Books, 1960.

Buber, Martin. *Between Man and Man.* New York: MacMillan Co., 1965.

Carroll, C. Edward. *The Professionalization of Education for Librarianship with Special Reference to the Years 1940-1960.* Metuchen, New Jersey: Scarecrow Press, 1970.

Carr-Saunders, A. M., and P. A. Wilson. *The Professions.* Oxford: Clarendon Press, 1933.

Corey, Stephen M. *Action Research to Improve School Practices.* New York: Teachers College, Columbia University, 1953.

Danton, J. Periam. *Education for Librarianship* (Unesco Public Library Manuals, I). Paris: Unesco, 1949.

Danton, J. Periam. *Education for Librarianship: Criticisms, Dilemmas and Proposals.* New York: Columbia University, School of Library Service, 1946.

Dewey, John. *Democracy and Education.* New York: Free Press, 1966.

Dewey, John. *Experience and Education.* New York: Collier Books, 1963.

Dewey, John. *How We Think.* Boston: D. C. Heath and Co., 1910.

Dewey, John. *Logic: The Theory of Inquiry.* New York: Henry Holt and Co., 1938.

Dewey, John. *Sources of a Science of Education.* New York: Horace Liveright, 1929.

Dubin, Robert, and Thomas C. Taveggia. *The Teaching-Learning Paradox: A Comparative Analysis of College Teaching Methods.* Eugene, Oregon: Center for the Advanced Study of Educational Administration, University of Oregon, 1968.

Flexner, Abraham. *Medical Education in the United States and Canada.* Boston: Merrymount Press, 1910.

Foshay, Arthur W., and James A. Hall, eds. *Research in Curriculum Improvement* (1957 Yearbook). Washington: Association for Supervision and Curriculum Development, 1957.

Gage, N. L., ed. *Handbook of Research on Teaching.* Chicago: Rand McNally and Co., 1963.

Gagne, Robert M. *The Conditions of Learning.* New York: Holt, Rinehart and Winston, 1965.

Good, Carter V. *Introduction to Educational Research.* New York: Appleton-Century-Crofts, 1959.

Gurin, Arnold. *Community Organization Curriculum in Graduate Social Work Education: Report and Recommendations.* New York: Council on Social Work Education, 1970.

Heiss, Ann M. *Challenges to Graduate Schools.* San Francisco: Josey-Bass, 1970.

Hollis, Ernest V., and Alice L. Taylor. *Social Work Education in the United States.* New York: Columbia University Press, 1951.

Hutchins, Robert M. *The University of Utopia.* Chicago: University of Chicago Press, 1953.

Kerlinger, Fred N. *Foundations of Behavioral Research.* New York: Holt, Rinehart and Winston, 1965.

Knapp, Patricia B. *The Monteith College Library Experiment.* New York: Scarecrow Press, 1966.

Leigh, Robert D., ed. *Major Problems in the Education of Librarians.* New York: Columbia University Press, 1954.

Lieberman, Myron. *The Future of Public Education.* Chicago: University of Chicago Press, 1960.

Metcalf, Keyes D., et al. *The Program of Instruction in Library Schools* (Illinois Contributions to Librarianship, No. 2). Urbana, Illinois: University of Illinois Press, 1943.

Mouly, George J. *The Science of Educational Research*, 2nd ed. New York: Van Nostrand, 1970.

National Society for the Study of Education. *Education for the Professions* (Sixty-first Yearbook, Part II). Chicago: University of Chicago Press, 1962.

O'Neill, William F., ed. *Selected Educational Heresies.* Glenview, Illinois: Scott, Foresman and Co., 1969.

Peters, R. S. *Ethics and Education.* Glenview, Illinois: Scott, Foresman and Co., 1967.

Polanyi, Michael. *Personal Knowledge.* Chicago: University of Chicago Press, 1958.

Reece, Ernest J. *The Curriculum in Library Schools.* New York: Columbia University Press, 1936.

Sabor, Josefa E. *Methods of Teaching Librarianship* (Unesco Manual for Libraries, 16). Paris: Unesco, 1969.

St. John, Francis R. *Internship in the Library Profession.* Chicago: American Library Association, 1938.

Shera, Jesse H. *The Foundations of Education for Librarianship.* New York: John Wiley and Sons, Inc., 1972.

Shumsky, Abraham. *The Action Research Way of Learning.* New York: Teachers College, Columbia University, 1958.

Stallmann, Esther L. *Library Internships: History, Purpose and a Proposal* (University of Illinois Graduate School of Library Science Occasional Papers, No. 37). Urbana, Illinois: University of Illinois Graduate School of Library Science, 1954.

Vann, Sarah K. *Training for Librarianship before 1923.* Chicago: American Library Association, 1961.

Waples, Douglas, and Ralph W. Tyler. *Research Methods and Teachers' Problems.* New York: MacMillan, 1930.

Wheeler, Joseph L. *Progress and Problems in Education for Librarianship.* New York: Carnegie Corporation of New York, 1946.

Whitney, Frederick L. *The Elements of Research.* New York: Prentice-Hall, 1946.

Williamson, Charles C. *Training for Library Service: A Report Prepared for the Carnegie Corporation of New York.* Boston: Merrymount Press, 1923.

PERIODICAL ARTICLES

Bartky, J. A. "The School of Education and the University," *Journal of Higher Education*, XXVI (May, 1955), 254-60.

Biddle, Bruce J. "Methods and Concepts in Classroom Research," *Review of Educational Research*, 37 (June, 1967), 337-57.

Boaz, Martha. "The Future of Library and Information Science Education," *Journal of Education for Librarianship*, 18 (Spring, 1978), 315-23.

Booker, Henry G. "University Education and Applied Science," *Science*, 141 (August 9, 1963), 486, 488, 575-76.

Braun, Richard L. "Practical Skills in the Law School Curriculum," *University of Dayton Law Review*, 2 (1977), 9-20.

Bruner, Jerome S. "On the Continuity of Learning," *Saturday Review of Education*, 1 (February 10, 1973), 21-24.

Cohen, Jerome. "Selected Constraints in the Relationship between Social Work Education and Practice," *Journal of Education for Social Work*, 13 (Winter, 1977), 3-7.

Cremin, Lawrence A. "The Education of the Educating Professions," *Research Bulletin: Horace Mann-Lincoln Institute*, 18 (March, 1978), 1-8.

Daily, Jay E. "Teaching the Rotten Core," *Library Journal*, 97 (May 15, 1972), 1778-83.

Downs, Robert B. "Quarters and Facilities: An Administrator's Point of View," *Journal of Education for Librarianship*, 7 (Fall, 1966), 84-89.

Ebert, Robert H. "Medical Education in the United States," *Daedalus: Journal of the American Academy of Arts and Sciences*, 106 (Winter, 1977), 171-84.

Finesilver, Sherman G. "The Tension between Practical and Theoretical Legal Education: A Judge's View of the Gap," *Brigham Young University Law Review*, 3 (1977), 1061-71.

Fingerson, Ronald L. "The Library Science Library: A Necessary Duplication," *Journal of Education for Librarianship*, 13 (Winter, 1973), 193-97.

Flanagan, John C. "The Critical Incident Technique," *Psychological Bulletin*, 51 (July, 1954), 327-58.

Flood, Barbara. "Some Thoughts on Graduate Education in Librarianship," *Journal of Education for Librarianship*, 12 (Fall, 1971), 133-37.

Gage, N. L., and W. R. Unruh. "Theoretical Formulations for Research on Teaching," *Review of Educational Research*, 37 (June, 1967), 358-70.

Galvin, Thomas J. "Problem-Oriented Approaches in the Education of Librarians," *Special Libraries*, 66 (January, 1975), 1-5.

Goldhor, Herbert. "Some Thoughts on the Curriculum of Library Schools," *School and Society*, LXVII (June 12, 1948), 433-36.

Grotzinger, Laura. "The Status of 'Practicum' in Graduate Library Schools," *Journal of Education for Librarianship*, 11 (Spring, 1971), 332-39.

Holley, Edward G. "Library Education and the Library Profession," *Texas Library Journal*, 53 (Spring, 1977), 72-80.

Jung, Steven M. "Evaluating Uses of Unconventional Measurement Techniques in an Educational System," *California Journal of Educational Research*, 22 (March, 1971), 48-57.

Kaser, David. "Library School Libraries," *Journal of Education for Librarianship*, 5 (Summer, 1964), 17-19.

Klempner, Irving M. "The New Imperatives: Decisions for Library School Curricula," *Special Libraries*, 67 (September, 1976), 409-14.

Knapp, Patricia B. "The Meaning of the Monteith College Library Program for Library Education," *Journal of Education for Librarianship*, 6 (Fall, 1965), 117-27.

Land, Brian. "Library School Quarters and Space – The Ideal," *Journal of Education for Librarianship*, 7 (Fall, 1966), 71-83.

Lawson, Barry R. "An Educational Simulation Model of Public Library Service," *Journal of Education for Librarianship*, 14 (Fall, 1973), 96-106.

Lee, Rex E. "Theory and Practice in Training for the Law; Thinking Like a Lawyer and Doing What He Does," *University of Dayton Law Review*, 2 (1977), 3-7.

Lieberman, Irving. "Library School Quarters for the Best Educational Practice," *Journal of Education for Librarianship*, 7 (Fall, 1966), 90-95.

Lukenbill, W. Bernard. "Content or Process: A Personal Look at Experiential Learning," *Journal of Education for Librarianship*, 16 (Winter, 1976), 195-204.

Lynch, Mary Jo, and George W. Whitbeck, "Work Experience and Observation in a General Reference Course – More on 'Theory vs. Practice,' " *Journal of Education for Librarianship*, 15 (Spring, 1975), 271-80.

Martell, Charles. "Age of Creative Insecurity: Student-Centered Learning," *Journal of Education for Librarianship*, 15 (Fall, 1974), 112-20.

Mayhew, Lewis B. "The Critical Incident Technique in Educational Evaluation," *Journal of Educational Research*, 49 (April, 1956), 591-98.

Mitchell, Sydney B. "The Pioneer Library School in Middle Age," *Library Quarterly*, 20 (October, 1950), 272-88.

Mitzel, Harold E. "Increasing the Impact of Theory and Research on Programs of Instruction," *Journal of Teacher Education*, 28 (November-December, 1977), 15-20.

Morehead, Joe. "Professional Education: The Theory-Practice Issue Reconsidered," *College Student Journal*, 7 (November-December, 1973), 71-82.

Morehead, Joe. "The Theory-Practice Problem and Library-Centered Library Education," *Journal of Education for Librarianship*, 14 (Fall, 1973), 119-28.

Patterson, Charles D. "The Seminar Method in Library Education," *Journal of Education for Librarianship*, 8 (Fall, 1967), 99-105.

Peterson, O. L., et al. "Appraisal of Medical Students' Abilities As Related to Training and Careers after Graduation," *New England Journal of Medicine*, 269 (1963), 1174-82.

Platt, John R. "Strong Inference," *Science*, 146 (April 1, 1970), 347-53.

Pope, Elspeth, and Katherine Armitage. "Status of Library School Librarians," *Journal of Education for Librarianship*, 11 (Spring, 1971), 340-43.

Price, Philip B., et al. "Measurement of Physician Performance," *Journal of Medical Education*, 39 (1964), 203-10.

Ramey, James W. "Simulation in Library Administration," *Journal of Education for Librarianship*, 8 (Fall, 1967), 85-93.

Schwartz, Morris S., and C. G. Schwartz. "Problems in Participant Observation," *American Journal of Sociology*, 60 (January, 1955), 343-53.

Shera, Jesse H. "Theory and Technique in Library Education," *Library Journal*, 85 (May 1, 1960), 1736-39.

Shuman, Bruce A. "Role-Playing and Simulation in Library School Courses," *The Library Scene*, 5 (September, 1976), 9-11.

Stevens, Norman D. "The Continuing Conflict," *Journal of Education for Librarianship*, 9 (Spring, 1969), 308-12.

Swank, Raynard C. "Sixth-Year Curricula and the Education of Library School Faculties," *Journal of Education for Librarianship*, 8 Summer, 1967), 14-19.

Taylor, Robert S. "Educational Breakaway," *American Libraries*, 10 (June, 1979), 364-68.

Van Deusen, Neil C. "Field Work in Accredited Library Schools," *College and Research Libraries*, VII (July, 1946), 249-55.

Vance, Kenneth E., et al. "Future of Library Education: 1975 Delphi Study," *Journal of Education for Librarianship*, 18 (Summer, 1977), 3-17.

Wasserman, Paul. "Professional Adaptation: Library Education Mandate," *Library Journal*, 95 (April 1, 1970), 1281-88.

Wilson, Pauline. "Impending Change in Library Education: Implications for Planning," *Journal of Education for Librarianship*, 18 (Winter, 1978), 159-74.

Witucke, Virginia. "Library School Policies toward Preprofessional Work Experience," *Journal of Education for Librarianship*, 16 (Winter, 1976), 162-72.

PAPERS AND PROCEEDINGS

Berelson, Bernard, ed. *Education for Librarianship*. Papers Presented at the Library Conference, University of Chicago, August 16-21, 1948. Chicago: American Library Association, 1949.

Bone, Larry Earl, ed. *Library Education: An International Survey.* Papers Presented at the International Conference on Librarianship Conducted by the University of Illinois Graduate School of Library Science, June 12-16, 1967. Urbana, Illinois: University of Illinois Graduate School of Library Science, 1968.

Bone, Larry Earl, ed. *Library School Teaching Methods: Courses in the Selection of Adult Materials.* Proceedings of a Conference on Library School Teaching Methods Held at the University of Illinois, September 8-11, 1968. Urbana, Illinois: University of Illinois Graduate School of Library Science, 1969.

Goldhor, Herbert, ed. *Education for Librarianship: The Design of the Curriculum of Library Schools.* Papers Presented at a Conference on the Design of the Curriculum of Library Schools Conducted by the University of Illinois Graduate School of Library Science, September 6-9, 1970. Urbana, Illinois: University of Illinois Graduate School of Library Science, 1971.

Goldstein, Harold, ed. *Library School Teaching Methods: Evaluation of Students.* Papers Presented at a Conference Conducted by the University of Illinois Graduate School of Library Science, April 9-12, 1967. Urbana, Illinois: University of Illinois Graduate School of Library Science, 1967.

Harm, Marvin P. "Changing from the Traditional Library to a Learning Laboratory," Paper Presented at the Institute on the Role of the Library School Library, Emory University, May 4, 1971. (Mimeographed.)

Klempner, Irving M., ed. *Conference on Education for Information Science—Strategies for Change in Library School Programs.* Proceedings of a Conference Held at the School of Library and Information Science, State University of New York at Albany, April 24-25, 1977, published in *Information Reports and Bibliographies*, 7, no. 4-5 (1978), 7-58.

Knapp, Patricia B. "The Library-Centered Library School." Paper Presented at a Conference on the Bibliographic Control of Library Science Literature, State University of New York at Albany, School of Library Science, April 19-20, 1968. (Mimeographed.)

Lee, Robert. "The Special Collection in Librarianship." Paper Presented at a Conference on the Bibliographic Control of Library Science Literature, State University of New York at Albany, School of Library Science, April 19-20, 1968. (Mimeographed.)

Smith, G. Kerry, ed. *Current Issues in Higher Education.* Proceedings of the 16th Annual National Conference on Higher Education. Washington: Association for Higher Education, 1961.

Swanson, Don R., ed. *The Intellectual Foundations of Library Education.* The Twenty-ninth Annual Conference of the Graduate Library School, University of Chicago, July 6-8, 1964. Chicago: University of Chicago Press, 1965.

PERSONAL AUTHOR INDEX

The entries in this index refer to passages in which individuals are treated as authors of specific works. Other references to these individuals are included in the Subject Index.

Anderson, L. G., 14
Asheim, L., 99, 111

Bartky, J. A., 12
Berelson, B., 13, 31
Biddle, B. J., 92, 114
Blauch, L. E., 12-13, 31
Boehm, W. W., 19
Booker, H. G., 17
Boyd, R. D., 54
Brown, G. S., 17-18
Bruner, J. S., 59, 80, 116
Buckland, M. K., 109-10

Carnovsky, L., 32
Carr-Saunders, A. M., 11
Carroll, C. E., 31-32
Caswell, H. L., 95
Churchwell, C. D., 31
Cohen, J., 20
Corey, S. M., 95, 96
Coughlin, V. L., 74

Daily, J. E., 70
Danton, J. P., 39-40, 58, 65, 68, 72, 85
Darley, J. G., 14
Dewey, J., 55, 93-94, 120
Downs, R. B., 87
Dubin, R., 55, 56
Dunkin, P., 54, 61, 69

Ebert, R. H., 17

Fingerson, R. L., 88
Flanagan, J. C., 91, 92
Flexner, A., 11, 31
Flood, B., 118

Gage, N. L., 114
Gagne, R. M., 73
Galvin, T. J., 59, 60, 67, 71
Getzels, J. W., 99, 115
Goldhor, H., 40
Good, C. V., 91, 96, 97-98
Grotzinger, L., 49
Gurin, A., 20

Harlow, N., 32
Harm, M. P., 112
Heiss, A. M., 14, 22, 113
Holley, E. G., 25
Hollis, E. V., 19
Hutchins, R. M., 12

Jung, S. M., 92

Kaser, D., 85, 86
Knapp, P. B., 80-85, 89, 91, 99-101, 119, 120

Lancour, H., 40
Land, B., 86, 87
Lanier, D. L., 88
Lawson, B. R., 61

Lee, R. E., 19, 87
Leigh, R. D., 42
Lieberman, I., 87
Lieberman, M., 20-22, 24, 44
Line, W., 67
Lukenbill, W. B., 79
Lynch, M. J., 72

Martell, C., 90
Mayhew, L. B., 29, 92-93
McConnell, T. R., 14
McGlothlin, W. J., 11, 13, 15-16
McGrath, E. J., 15, 16, 23, 24, 25, 88-89
Metcalf, K. D., 40, 41, 57, 64, 66, 68-69
Miller, G. E., 16-17, 24
Monroe, M. E., 85-86
Morison, R. S., 90

Niederhauser, M., 87

Osborn, A. D., 110, 118

Patterson, C. D., 66-67
Peters, R. S., 74, 79-80
Polanyi, M., 94
Poole, W. F., 30

Ramey, J. W., 60, 61
Reece, E. J., 35-37, 44, 47-48, 49, 56, 62, 64, 65-66, 69, 89
Rogers, C. R., 90
Rothstein, S., 29, 38, 45, 46

Sabor, J. E., 61, 62, 65, 70, 73
St. John, F. R., 38-39, 42
Schwartz, C. G., 96-97
Schwartz, M. S., 96-97
Shaffer, K., 58
Shera, J. H., 24-25, 54, 109, 112
Shuman, B. A., 61
Stallmann, E. L., 42-44
Stevens, N. D., 87
Swank, R. C., 32, 48, 119
Swanson, R. W., 110

Taveggia, T. C., 55, 56
Taylor, A. L., 19
Taylor, R. S., 112, 113
Travers, R. M. W., 71
Truax, N. C., 87
Tyler, R. W., 95

Unruh, W. R., 114

Van Deusen, N. C., 41, 42
Vann, S. K., 31

Wallen, N. E., 71
Waples, D., 95
Wasserman, P., 117-18
Wetmore, R. B., 87
Wheeler, J. L., 40-41, 58
Whitbeck, G. W., 72
Whitney, F. L., 95
Williamson, C. C., 30, 31, 32, 33-35, 44, 47, 49, 57, 89, 116
Wilson, L. R., 31
Wilson, P. A., 11

SUBJECT INDEX

Other references to individuals listed in this index can be found in the Personal Author Index.

Accreditation, 31
Action research, 95-96
American Bar Association, 18
American Library Association, 38, 39
Association of American Library Schools, 37

Bartky, J. A., 12, 13
Billings, J. S., 30
Blauch, L. E., 12-13
Board of Education for Librarianship (ALA), 38
Booker, H. G., 17
Brown, G. S., 17-18

Carnovsky, L., 32
Case method, *see* Modes of instruction
Chicago University, 42
Class discussion, *see* Modes of instruction
Class presentation, 71
Class presentation (Reece), 35-36, 55, 57-62
See also work contacts (Reece)
Columbia University, 30, 35
Concurrence in professional education, 89
Critical incident technique, 91-93, 98-99
analytic units, 92, 101
phenomenal units, 92, 101

Danton, J. P., 39-40
Delphi-Method survey, 7
Delphi Study, 46
Dewey, J., 55, 93-94
Dewey, M., 30, 31, 46-47
Division of the Social Sciences (Chicago University), 42
Dubin, R., 55-56
"Dynamic-heuristic" model, 115

Face-to-face instruction, *see* Modes of instruction
Field practice, 33
Field work (Metcalf), 41
Field work (Reece), 36, 48, 54-55
See also Work contacts (Reece)
Field work (Van Deusen), 42
Field work (Williamson), 33, 34-35
Fingerson, R. L., 88
Flexner, A., 11, 13, 17, 31
Forms (Reece), *see* Work contacts (Reece)

Galvin, T. J., 59-60

Harvard Business School, 59
Heiss, A. M., 14
Hutchins, R. M., 12, 13

Independent study, 56, 62-64, 71-72
supervised, 62-63
unsupervised, 63-64
Individualized instruction, 114
Information science, 109-13
Information transfer, 109
Inquiry model (Dewey), 93-94, 98-99
International Conference on Librarianship, 45
Internships, 16-17, 21-22, 24, 34, 89
defined, 43
supervision of, 38-39, 41, 43, 48

Knapp, P. B., 80, 81, 83-84, 91, 99-100

Laboratory work, *see* Field work, Internships, Modes of instruction
Laboratory work (Reece), 35-36, 55, 69
   See also Work contacts (Reece)
Lanier, D. L., 88
Lecture method, *see* Modes of instruction
Legal education, 18-19
Liberal education, 11
Library-centered library education, 79-106
   content of, 81
   justification of, 88-89
   learning strategies, 90-94
   methods of instruction, 82-83
   teaching strategies, 95-99
Library education, criticisms of, 32
Library school libraries, 84-89
Library School of the New York Public Library, 30
Lieberman, M., 34-35
Literature of librarianship, 81, 89, 99-100

McGlothlin, W. J., 12
McGrath, E. J., 23
   criteria for planning curricula, 23-24, 25, 35, 74
Medical education, 11, 20, 21, 34, 117
Metcalf, K. D., 57, 69
Modes of instruction, 54-78, 107
   case study, 59-61, 67, 71
   class discussion, 58, 71
   face-to-face, 55-56, 89
   laboratory work, 33, 67-70, 73-74, 89
   lecture, 57-58, 61-62, 71
   observation, 64-65, 72
   problems, 62-64, 71
   projects, 65-67, 72
   seminar, 66-67, 89
   seminar-laboratory, 89, 101, 118
   simulation, 61
   students teaching students, 61

New York Public Library, 30

Observation, *see* Modes of instruction
Observation (Reece), 36, 55, 64
   See also Work contacts (Reece)

Participant observation, 96-98
Practical work, 33, 69-70
   See also Field Work, Internships
   criticisms of, 46
Practice, definitions, 6-7
Practice work, 33
   See also Field work, Internships
Problems, *see* Modes of instruction
Problems (Reece), 36, 55, 62
   See also Work contacts (Reece)
Professional activity, 21, 40, 84
Professional education, 11-28
   concurrence in, 89
Professionalization in education, 13, 23, 31, 47
Projects, *see* Modes of instruction
Projects (Reece), 35, 36, 65-66
   See also Work contacts (Reece)

Ramey, J. W., 60-61
Reasoning (Dewey), 94
Reece, E. J., 35, 54-55, 57, 89
   See also Work contacts (Reece)
Reece's five forms, *see* Work contacts (Reece)
Rensselaer Polytechnic Institute, 17
Research-demonstration centers, 19
Rothstein, S., 45-46

St. John, F. R., 38-39
School of Library Economy (Columbia), 30
Seminars, *see* Modes of instruction
Simulation, *see* Modes of instruction
Social work education, 19-20
Specialization in education, 13
Stallmann, E. L., 42-44
Student-centered teaching (Martell), 90
Student teaching, 21

Taveggia, T. C., 55-56
Teacher education, 20-21
Technology and library education, 111
Theory, definitions, 6-7

Unity, 5
University of Illinois Graduate School of Library Science, 45
University of Texas Graduate School of Library Science, 44-45

Van Deusen, N. C., 41-42
Vocational education, 11

Wheeler, J. L., 40-41
Williamson, C. C., 30, 33-35, 37, 47, 57,
  89
Winsor, J., 30
Work contacts, 45
Work contacts (Reece), 35-36, 49, 54-55, 56